WALKING WITH GOD IN THE BACKWOODS

I hope you enjoy the story of my family. May God bless you and yours.

Mabel Margaret Bufford

First Assembly of God
P.O. box 302
Weiner, AR 72479

WALKING WITH GOD IN THE BACKWOODS

Mabel Margaret Motes Bufford

TATE PUBLISHING
AND ENTERPRISES, LLC

Walking with God in the Backwoods
Copyright © 2016 by Mabel Margaret Motes Bufford. All rights reserved.

No part of this publication may be reproduced, stored in a retrieval system or transmitted in any way by any means, electronic, mechanical, photocopy, recording or otherwise without the prior permission of the author except as provided by USA copyright law.

Scripture quotations are taken from the *Holy Bible, King James Version*, Cambridge, 1769. Used by permission. All rights reserved.

This book is designed to provide accurate and authoritative information with regard to the subject matter covered. This information is given with the understanding that neither the author nor Tate Publishing, LLC is engaged in rendering legal, professional advice. Since the details of your situation are fact dependent, you should additionally seek the services of a competent professional.

The opinions expressed by the author are not necessarily those of Tate Publishing, LLC.

Published by Tate Publishing & Enterprises, LLC
127 E. Trade Center Terrace | Mustang, Oklahoma 73064 USA
1.888.361.9473 | www.tatepublishing.com

Tate Publishing is committed to excellence in the publishing industry. The company reflects the philosophy established by the founders, based on Psalm 68:11,
"The Lord gave the word and great was the company of those who published it."

Book design copyright © 2016 by Tate Publishing, LLC. All rights reserved.
Cover design by Niño Carlo Suico
Interior design by Mary Jean Archival

Published in the United States of America

ISBN: 978-1-68254-701-4
Biography & Autobiography / Personal Memoirs
15.11.17

To all who have loved me.
To my sisters, Kathy and Audrey Motes, whose untimely
deaths were a tragedy from which we will not recover.
For they have taken a part of us with them.

Contents

Preface 9

Introduction.. 11

1 Where He Leads 15
2 That Glad Reunion Day 27
3 Tell Me the Old, Old Story... 35
4 Amazing Grace 59
5 A New Name in Glory, 1948 75
6 I'll Be List'ning, 1955.. 93
7 The Old-Time Religion, 1956 101
8 Gathering Home, 1957 111
9 When the Saints Go Marching In, 1958.................. 123
10 Where Could I Go but to the Lord,
   Easter Sunday, 1960 151
11 No Tears in Heaven, 1960 161

12	Hold to God's Unchanging Hand, 1961	181
13	When the Roll Is Called Up Yonder	193
14	I'll Fly Away	213
15	I'll Meet You in the Morning, 1994	253
16	This World Is Not My Home	261
17	Love Lifted Me	273
18	Wonderful Words of Life	283
19	We'll Understand It Better By and By	287
20	I'll Live On	293

Preface

IT IS MY DESIRE THAT this book will be a candid celebration of the grace of God that sustained us in our wilderness—known as the backwoods—where *He* walked among us. To God be the glory.

Introduction

THEY WERE NOT THE "GOOD ole days," therefore, I will not suggest that we go back to the way things were. We cannot go back and we have no desire to. Too much has changed, and much of it is for the better. I still like peace, silence, and solitude, and that is a part of the past I have chosen to keep. In our modern times, we have so much "racket" that it is more difficult to maintain a life of prayer and insightful thought. Though it is harder now, it is not impossible. Fortunately, God has not changed. He will still respond to anyone who calls upon him.

It takes a conscious effort to cultivate a meaningful relationship with our creator. We pick our priorities for each day, and our life is the sum total of our days. To wish away a single day is to wish our life away. To waste our day is to destroy a portion of what was once our future. Life is fragile and temporary at best. Even a long life is not long enough.

All scriptures used in this book are from the King James Version. That was the only version available to us as children, and we naturally adapted to it. We were unaware that there were other versions. Yes, it was hard to understand, but we mined the diamonds and golden nuggets of truth from the more difficult source as the Holy Spirit gave insight and understanding. A simple Bible verse that should be easily understood caused me to feel a bit of confusion. It is the one in Hebrews 11:6: "But without faith it is impossible to please him: for he that cometh to God must believe that he is, and that he is a rewarder of them that diligently seek him." When such bad things happen to good people, it caused me to wonder: what are the rewards on earth for the righteous? I understand that heaven is to be the reward for Christ's believers for all eternity, but I have a tendency toward desiring rewards in this life as well.

Our earthly rewards are not always what we expect them to be. Earthly rewards do not always come when we expect them to come and in the way we expect. The rewards we hope for in the *here* and *now* are success, prosperity, and pleasure. Reality is, "in this world ye shall have tribulation" (John 16:33). My parents and grandparents had their share of tribulation as we all must. If this life is a test—competition between good and evil—the winners are those who remain *faithful* while doing the *will of the Father* and *endure to the end* (Matt. 7:21, 10:22, 25:21).

There is something about that word *endure* that I don't like. No one has to endure pleasure or prosperity or success.

Walking with God in the Backwoods

It may be that the suffering in Job's life was not just a one-time event involving one man and one family. It may be an example which reflects life on earth for all mankind. While reading the scriptures, I watched for the earthly rewards for those who pleased Him. One of the first things I noticed is that God does not remove the struggle.

It is generally understood that I am the product of my environment. To understand me, you may need to meet my parents who were responsible for setting the tone in our home during my childhood. You must also be introduced to my grandparents whose influence was felt indirectly because they were the ones who influenced my parents. For this reason, my story covers more than one hundred years and highlights three generations—from my grandparents, David and Mary Motes, who were born in the 1880s to the death of my parents, Levi and Eva Motes, which occurred after the turning of the year 2000.

Our two most significant dates are birth and death, and life is our personal experience in the short span of time between those two dates. Each life has its own adventures which cannot be recaptured and neither can they be duplicated. The life of each individual is as a story told.

> The Lord is nigh unto all them that call upon him,
> to all that call upon him in truth.

—Psalms 145:18

1

Where He Leads

Columbiaville, Michigan, 2014

CHECKING THE MAILBOX IN HOPE of a personal letter still registers as a delight among older retired people like me and my husband Sam. Most often, we get only junk mail or bills. But we go back each day with high hopes that things will be different today. It's a lot like going fishing. Occasionally, we get a nibble. We pull out a birthday card addressed in handwritten script only to find it is from the car dealership or from our insurance company. Sometimes, we get lucky. October 7, 2014, was my lucky day.

Nestled among the many bills and junk mail pulled from the mailbox was a personal letter. It had a return address from Katie Keller, the wife of my childhood Sunday school teacher.

Mabel Margaret Motes Bufford

Still being active in the same church that was once *our* church, Katie sent an announcement for the homecoming reunion at the Weiner First Assembly of God Church.

When I was a teenager, Katie was a young mother, and she taught my little brothers and sisters in Sunday school class. I had not seen or heard from her in forty-seven years.

With great excitement, I read my invitation; the homecoming event would be on November 9, 2014. For some unknown reason, I felt compelled to go back to Weiner, Arkansas, to visit my childhood church for this special occasion. Sam didn't feel well enough to travel but was in agreement with my going. Right away, I purchased an airplane ticket and made preparations to go without him.

—⧟—

Weiner, Arkansas, 1967

It has been forty-seven years since I graduated from high school in Weiner, Arkansas, on May 15, 1967. I remember it as a beautiful spring day and the cotton planted in the field next to our house was coming up nicely. Upon assessing the crop, my dad said it was "a good stand of cotton."

My parents, Levi and Eva Motes, and I were home alone on graduation day. Being near the middle in a family of seven children, I was unaccustomed to getting individual attention from my parents. It was their habit to deal with us as a group most often. It was a strange feeling yet luxurious to be at home while my younger siblings, Joe, Mildred, and Andrew, were required to be in school.

After my dad went about his business with farmwork, I asked my mother to take a photograph of me in my graduation cap and gown on my special day. I don't know if she had ever taken a photo before. It was Andrew's camera, and we hardly knew how to use it. He had obtained it by mail order. Our family had never owned a camera before, so we had very few photographs of our family. A few other people had taken pictures of us and had given them to us throughout the years. We had few close friends or relatives that could afford a camera and film and especially the high cost of getting film developed.

A week after graduation, I left Arkansas with my teenage boyfriend, Sam Bufford. He had graduated from Grubbs High School in 1965, where he was known as Sammy. Though he had moved away with his family, we maintained a sweet courtship by mail while I finished high school.

Taylor, Michigan, 1967

Sam and his sister Angela drove from Taylor, Michigan, where his family lived to pick me up. I was eager to start a new life in a new location. Arriving in Michigan, we planned an inexpensive wedding, which would take place in the Bufford family's modest living room. We allowed ten days to make all our plans

Mabel Margaret Motes Bufford

and arrangements. We chose a date in the near future because we were aware that it did not look dignified for me to live in the same house with Sam without the benefit of marriage. Planning for a Friday evening ceremony would give us a whole weekend together before Sam had to return to work.

The change in my world was so sudden and drastic that I could hardly take it all in. Since our residence was in Wayne County, we were required to go to the heart of downtown Detroit to apply for a marriage license at the City-County Building. This was the beginning of culture shock for me.

If Sam had many fears about navigating the heavy inner city traffic, he did not let me know of it. I was by nature a fearful person and had enough fears for both of us. Sam had learned his way around somewhat, and he was my brave knight in shining armor.

On the first weekend that Sam was off work, we went to a local jewelry store and bought the prettiest wedding bands we could get for the least amount of money. All the money we had which could be spent on the wedding and a place to live was a little over $300. Our search for a low-cost apartment yielded no results. We were destined to live with Sam's family for two months while we saved money and continued the search.

I had sewn a simple white dress in the previous days and baked my own three-tiered wedding cake on the day of our ceremony. Since the wedding plans required little from Sam, he went to work as usual on that momentous day. By the time he got home and got cleaned up, his aunt and uncle had arrived with their family of three children. They had come to Michigan from Drasco, Arkansas, for Mr. Ramer to work a summer job.

The Wedding

Though I had not been acquainted with the Ramer family previously, Sam's Uncle Parm agreed to take the place of my dad during the wedding ceremony to give me away. He and his wife, Mae, were pleased to be our witnesses and to sign our marriage license. Also in attendance were Sam's older half brother, Kenneth (from Mr. Bufford's previous marriage), Kenneth's wife, Sharon, and their two little girls, Sherry and Kim. With Sam being the oldest of Wincie and Dalton's nine children, the room was filled to capacity. Angela stood beside me as my maid of honor, and Kenneth was Sam's best man. Mr. Bufford, having been a licensed Baptist minister, gladly performed the ceremony for us. Even though none of my relatives could be there, it was a nice little family affair. Sam and I became husband and wife on June 2, 1967.

Identity

When I left Arkansas, I left my family, friends, and all that was familiar to me. In a moment of time, Mabel Motes from

Weiner High School became Margaret Bufford in Michigan. Like removing a tattered garment, I planned to shed the shame of poverty in a new land of possibilities. Along with changing my address and marital status, my identity was officially changed. I had suddenly become a part of a new family and had many new relatives. It was like being placed in the Federal Witness Protection Program. The only difference is, I did it to myself.

The quality and direction of our lives are the result of our choices. If we are wise, we will pray about our decisions before we make those choices. I am blessed that I chose a Christian young man to date and to marry. With Sam's family being established in a church, it increased the probability that we too would build our future on the same firm foundation. The weekend that we were married, we went to church on Sunday morning. Regular church attendance was such an ingrained habit in us that it was automatic. We went to church with the Bufford family in a public school gymnasium that a small congregation had rented. I had the encouragement that I needed to keep growing in spiritual disciplines. Keeping my Christian identity was easy.

—⟋⟍—

Homesick for Arkansas

I'd only been gone six months, but it felt like six years. Homesickness for my family in Arkansas began taking a toll

Walking with God in the Backwoods

on me. That was the deciding factor in Sam taking a week of vacation time from the small manufacturing shop where he was working as a welder. He drove me back to Arkansas to visit those I had so longed to see.

It was refreshing to step back into our former world and travel familiar country roads again. I enjoyed the love of my family and went to church with them at my childhood church. I had attended there from the age of nine until I left home at eighteen. My older sister, Audrey, and my younger brother, Joe, were in Sunday school class with Sam and me on that day. It would be the last time we would be in class together. Cleveland Keller was still teaching the teenagers and the young adults' class. Little had changed there—but I had changed. Maybe I had matured a little.

How could I have known that I would never again attend the Harmony Grove Assembly of God Church nestled in the little grove of trees? I enjoyed my little country church. Even the name of it was special to me. Both of the words *harmony* and *grove* are beautiful words that inspire lovely thoughts. We just called it Harmony Grove. We didn't bother to add the Assembly of God part to that. It was there that I met the lover of my soul at the age of thirteen and trusted Jesus Christ to be my Savior. It was also there that I met the love of my life when I was sixteen years of age. Sam, his parents, and his siblings attended church with my family at Harmony Grove from the summer of 1965 until they moved to Michigan in the summer of 1966. What a special place that church had in my heart.

—⁓—

New Church in Michigan, 1967

My allegiance shifted gradually from the Harmony Grove church to the new congregation in Michigan. Within a few months, they had accumulated sufficient funds to make a down payment on a building. The pastor found an old building in the town of Ypsilanti, which was in our price range but would need some repairs.

The bank required the church to select four men from the congregation to sign papers as a guarantee that the payments would be made. At the young age of twenty-one, Sam was among the men who signed to buy the church building. Sam's dad and his brother Kenneth also chose to sign for the debt of the church. They didn't seem to be aware of the fact that this was an extraordinary act. They were just doing what felt like the right thing to do at the time.

Being the only woman in the room while the men signed the legal papers caused me to feel uncomfortable. I didn't realize that other wives would not choose to be there. Since church business was considered "men's business," I felt as out of place as a fly on the wall. Maybe I was supposed to be there to record this information for the sake of family history. As far as I know, the three Bufford men never spoke of it again. This is an important part of the Bufford children's Christian heritage that I determined should be passed down to future generations.

When it was time to work on the church building, Sam and I donated our labor one Saturday. Standing on a ladder, Sam stapled insulation in the ceiling and walls of the foyer while I unrolled it and passed it along to him. I was still a teenager and had never even seen insulation before. I wasn't there because of my knowledge and experience. Sam and I were newlyweds, and we wanted to spend the day together. I was in the position of having to make a quick transition from being a girl to being a woman. I was learning to be more than a wife and companion; I was learning to be a helpmate.

Though Sam was only a year and a half older than me, he was far more mature than I was. He was a good worker and respected among the men. He had integrity and the sweet nature of a Southern gentleman. I was very proud of him.

Working beside Sam at the church set precedence for our marriage. We discovered that our happiest times were the result of working together toward a common goal. We still enjoy seeing the steady progress of home-modernizing projects and love the sense of fulfillment that comes when the job is done. We find that working together is more exhilarating than most sources of entertainment and amusement.

Visiting the Ypsilanti Church, 1990

About twenty years after we left the church in Ypsilanti, the Lord arranged an occasion for us to go back there one more time. We were attending a small church in Romulus, near the Detroit Metropolitan airport, which did not have baptismal facilities. Our pastor needed to borrow another church so he could baptize the youngest two of our four children, Sammy and Krista. Imagine our surprise when the church that agreed to loan us their facilities was the very church we had helped to establish in Ypsilanti. Neither pastor was aware of our history with the Ypsilanti church. After moving to another area, we had lost all connection to that part of our past.

Farewell to Harmony Grove, 1994

About seven years after I moved to Michigan, my parents retired from sharecropping and moved to the town of Tuckerman. The forty acres of fertile farmland where I grew up was owned by my maternal grandmother, Flora Della Clark West. In her eighties, Grandma West sold the farm so she could give an inheritance to each of her heirs. To our dismay, the next owner turned several acres of the property into a catfish farm with several large ponds of water. Eventually, the business was abandoned, and the property was for sale again. The standing water become breeding grounds for mosquitoes and venomous snakes called water moccasins.

Walking with God in the Backwoods

Old houses in the community had been torn down, and the younger generation had gone away to search for jobs in big cities. The few people left in the congregation at Harmony Grove voted to move the struggling church to the town of Weiner. They had good reason. The land was low in the area of Harmony Grove, and country roads would sometimes flood, making it hard to reach the church after a heavy rain. The move was completed in November of 1994. At some point, the name was changed to Weiner First Assembly of God. Eventually, the vacant church building was removed, and the property returned to farmland.

Harmony Grove was the church where my siblings and I got most of our Christian training. The church did a fine job for the Motes children who endured stark poverty in the rural community near Flag Slough. Like good shepherds who are committed to the well-being of their sheep, the teachers watched for our souls, loved us, and prayed for us. Though we were very poor, they were happy to have us there. They made us feel accepted and acceptable. How sad that such a beloved country church would be in existence for only forty years.

> O give thanks unto the Lord; for he is good;
> for his mercy endureth for ever.
>
> —1 Chronicles 16:34

That Glad Reunion Day

November 9, 2014

My younger sister, Mildred, and her husband, William (Bill) Mount, attended the reunion service with me at Weiner First Assembly of God. We were excited to see several old friends from the past. We used this occasion to remember those who had once been a part of us but had been taken by death. They, like the heroes of faith, are now with the Lord. We grieved for our siblings whose young lives had been cut short. Even as children, they had a hand in helping to pioneer a church.

There were eleven ladies and two men present who had attended the church with us between the years of 1958 and 1967. We will be forever linked to them by having been church pioneers at the same time and place. The famous preacher and author A. W. Tozer said, "We can be in our day what the heroes of faith were in their day—but remember at the time they didn't know they were heroes."

Katie Keller is now a widow and in her mid-seventies. She and her husband, Cleveland, will be remembered in the local church history as heroes of the faith. Like a good hostess, Katie fluttered about as she greeted each visitor. She was so excited to see all her old friends. All the work she had done to help plan, organize, and contact people had paid off.

Katie was eager to show us a book she had written with the help of her daughter, Marie, entitled *My Little Country Church*. It was her memories of Harmony Grove printed especially for her grown children and close friends. I wanted a copy of the book, but only fifteen copies had been made, and there were none left.

Katie had prepared a display of old photos from the past for all to enjoy. She was one of the few people we knew who had owned a camera back then. She had a great love for documenting the events of her life with photographs. My siblings were in one of the old group photos of the primary Sunday school class. "I want a copy of that one," I told Katie, for it included my youngest sister Kathryn. Kathy had died at the age of four, shortly after the photo was taken.

The Wilderness Song

An elder in the Weiner church, Sam Wells, opened the service with a personal testimony. He sang the opening song as the worship team accompanied him on their instruments. How fitting that he chose to sing "I've Never Been This Homesick Before." Those of us who had experienced the crushing blows of homesickness could identify. The song portrayed the mindset of a godly saint who is ready to make the transition from this world to the heavenly realm. Many of us have now joined the ranks of senior citizens and are coming to grips with our own mortality. The realization of our age is shocking. We are grieving ahead of time for the passing of our own life as we are nearing our earthly departure.

"This world has been a wilderness" was a sad line in the song. Clutching tissue and dabbing at my eyes, I looked across the auditorium to see if there were others visibly moved to tears. There were none. *I'm not like other people*, I thought. It's often embarrassing to be different.

"I feel teary," I whispered to Pat Easter, the childhood friend who sat to my right. She smiled slightly. She probably felt it too; she just managed to keep her composure better than I did.

We were privileged to hear a message in tongues. That is an experience unique to Pentecostal believers. The Sectional Presbyter and guest speaker, Rev. Keith Underhill, proclaimed a powerful word from the Lord God by the gift of interpretation. The message began something like, "Just as I was with you in 1954, I am with you today…"

Those words must have been most comforting for Gwen Clark, who had been there on July 29, 1954, when she and several of her relatives signed the original papers to apply for affiliation with the Assemblies of God. Those were certainly reassuring words to those of us who had labored less years and loved the Harmony Grove church.

Approaching eighty-five years of age, Gwen was in fragile health. She has suffered great sorrow as death claimed not only her dearly loved husband but two of her adult children, Sandra Kay and Acel Jr. Sitting for such a prolonged amount of time was difficult for Gwen. As soon as the church service was over, she was eager to be driven to her home.

As she walked toward the car, Gwen stopped on the sidewalk to be included in a few photos with her three daughters and longtime friend, Katie. She chose not to join us for the meal that had been prepared for all. There were so many people in attendance that tables and chairs had to be set up in the parking lot to accommodate the overflow crowd.

—⚒—

Cycles of Time

It is very unusual to have three significant anniversaries in the same year. On November 9, 2014, not only did we celebrate *twenty* years in the new church building in town,

Walking with God in the Backwoods

but it had been *sixty* years since the original church called Harmony Grove was officially launched in 1954. It had been *one hundred* years since the Assemblies of God denomination was officially organized in 1914. The year of our Lord 2014 was a special year of celebration. Only God knows the true significance of these three anniversaries.

In the Bible, we find that God often used cycles of time and preferred to use certain numbers. One of the numbers frequently used was *forty*. We noticed that the year 1914 when the Assemblies of God were officially organized as a denomination until 1954 when a group of Pentecostal believers applied to form a church in the abandoned Harmony Grove school house was *forty* years. The time from the year 1954 when the country church was established until 1994 when that congregation got an upgrade and moved to town was another *forty* years. There is no way any person could have manipulated the numbers to organize this; it has the fingerprints of God all over it. It was an honor to be included in the great work God has done and is continuing to do there.

The church, now called Weiner First Assembly of God, is ordained of God for His glory. I'll be eager to see what He is up to. If this pattern continues, I will expect the church to switch gears again in the year 2034. If I'm still alive, and there is a chance I will be, I'll be watching. Maybe I'll be there to visit.

For the Lord thy God hath blessed thee in all the works of thy hand: he knoweth thy walking through this great

Mabel Margaret Motes Bufford

> wilderness: these forty years the Lord thy God hath been
> with thee; thou hast lacked nothing.

> —Deuteronomy 2:7

—⟋ℳ⟍—

A Time to Grieve

Immediately after the meal, the church ladies packed away the leftover food, and the men carried the tables and chairs back to their rightful place. Guest musicians scurried about in the auditorium as they set up their instruments and equipment. The Velvet Ridge Singers were preparing to give a two-hour concert in the afternoon.

Mildred, Bill, and I excused ourselves from the festivities. We chose rather to spend the remainder of the day visiting the graves of our loved ones. Upon arriving at the Clark Cemetery, about a mile from Uno, we were surprised to find that two other people from the reunion, Noel and Geraldine Madison, had made the same decision. They too had skipped the Gospel concert portion of the festivities to honor their dead and mourn their passing.

Among the relatives buried at the Clark Cemetery are our maternal grandparents, Samuel and Della West. Our little sister, Kathy, was buried beside them. Bill drove Mildred and me to three other cemeteries that day without becoming the least bit impatient with us. My parents, Levi and Eva Motes, are buried near Bradford within three miles of Mildred and Bill's residence.

It doesn't matter how old you may be when both of your parents are gone, there is a sense of being an orphan. Having a mother-in-law or a father-in-law helps; at least there is someone to call you daughter or son, and you have someone to call Mom and Dad. With both the mother-in-law and father-in-law gone as well, the sense of being an orphan is even more pronounced.

A Time to Regret

Oh how Mildred and I wished that we had asked more questions about the childhood of our parents and grandparents. We should have written down their history, their observations, and their advice and kept it for future generations. Along with the grieving for our elders is the regret of having squandered opportunities.

Mildred and Bill, and Sam and I are in our sixties, and we have no living parents-in-law or parents. Their passing happened sooner than we expected. We thought we had plenty of time to ask questions about family history. Now we must scramble to get our memories on paper before the eyesight dims and memories fade. As we are getting older, we find that our name, our heritage, and our testimony are among the more important things that belong to us exclusively.

Our advice to young people is to start asking the important questions now. Once the older generation is gone, it's too late. Our generation assumed that the skills of our grandparents had become irrelevant. In our modern industrialized society, technology now beckons as the new frontier.

We underestimated the value of our parents' wisdom and knowledge when we discarded their simple lifestyle. Now, we are concerned for our children and our grandchildren who would be ill prepared to live without technology. While there is time, learn from older people who are willing and able to teach. If the electrical grid should fail and the rule of law should break down, we may once again need to access primitive skills for living a simple life.

> To every thing there is a season, and a time to every purpose under the heaven.

—Ecclesiastes 3:1

Tell Me the Old, Old Story

Alabama, 1884

MARY URSLEY EDGAR, MY GRANDMOTHER, was born in Lamar, Alabama, on October 13, 1884. Little is known about her because she grew up in the care of an aunt and uncle, Mr. and Mrs. John Edgar. I was told that Mary was less than five feet in height and wore a size 5 shoe. In fairy tale fashion, the slender wisp of a girl with dark hair fell in love with a handsome young man.

David Edward Motes, far from being a prince, just happened to be two years younger than Mary. He was born on September 22, 1886, in Franklin, Alabama. David was sixteen years old and Mary was eighteen when they were married on a beautiful spring day, on April 12, 1903.

David and Mary's firstborn child was a boy who was either stillborn or died in early infancy and next came Annie, Jesse, and Ellie. Toward the middle of the ten children they produced was Levi, who would become my father. The younger children among his siblings were William, Helen, Thomas, James (Jim), and John Henry. David was pleased to tell others that he was one of seven sons and he had seven sons. Having daughters was less important to most men in those days. It would be many more years before Mary's three daughters could enjoy the rights, the status, and the privileges that were bestowed upon her sons.

Spiritual Heritage

There had been a great spiritual renewal in the late 1880s, and David and Mary had received good religious training during their childhood. As a young man, David had learned to read music at a General Baptist church, but he played no musical instrument. He amazed people with his ability to sing unfamiliar songs by knowing the sound of shape notes. Throughout David's adult life, he carried a tuning fork and was delighted to give lessons for reading musical notes in the hymn book. He was eager to teach singing and directed the choir when they stayed in one location long enough.

David and Mary were good singers who enjoyed singing the familiar hymns. Their talent opened a few doors of opportunity for them as they moved about. Though Mary was a tiny lady, she was blessed with a big voice. It was reported she had such talent that a piano was once tuned to her voice. Being involved with the choir and teaching others to read shape notes seemed to be David's primary interest in church as he grew older. It was Mary who had a heart after God and provided spiritual training for their nine children.

Ancestry

Mary informed her children that she was Black Dutch. This was a term used by some people to cover up the American Indian in their heritage. Children who were known to be part Indian were disrespected and unwelcomed in the country schools. Everyone except the Indians had their origin in another country. It was a matter of great pride for some people and gave them social status if their ancestors were from an acceptable European nation. Though David considered himself *Irish*, his grandmother was an American Indian. Both the native Indians and the Irish were held in low esteem.

Working on the Railroad

David was familiar with the hard work on the railroad where he helped to put down the iron rails. He told his sons that it took six men to carry a rail which weighed eleven hundred pounds and was twenty-two feet in length.

It took a multitude of men and a great amount of effort to build the railroads that snaked through the forests, around the mountains, and across the rivers. To earn a regular wage, David had few choices besides the grueling work on the railroad. Although it was known to be another hard job, he chose rather to work in the timber trade at sawmills. Either occupation required that he uproot his family frequently to move along with the job. During times that Mary was expecting a new baby, David would stay behind. He could partner with a friend to cut trees with a two-man crosscut saw and hew railroad ties with a broad-axe and sell them to the railroad.

Birth of Fifth Child—Robert Levi Motes

The Motes family had traveled to Gattman, Mississippi, while following the timber industry. Levi was born there on February 19, 1911. Like the Israelites who made laps in the wilderness, the Motes family eventually headed back to Phil Campbell, Alabama, which was a familiar place with family and friends. Levi had fair skin with freckles, red hair, and deep dimples. He was quite sickly all through his childhood and was short in stature. As it was with a litter of puppies, an unusually small child in a family was sometimes referred to affectionately as the "runt of the bunch."

Moonshine

During a desperate period of unemployment, even law-abiding citizens could be tempted to build a still and produce moonshine. Like modern drug dealing, making and selling moonshine was considered easy money.

A story was told of an illegal business venture which resulted in David being arrested for bootlegging. His incarceration would place an impossible burden on Mary to support their little family while David was behind bars. Compassionate law officials arranged to provide employment for Mary. She gladly accepted a job working in the kitchen and cooking for the prisoners until David was released. Mary's older boys, Jesse and Levi, were delighted to be given the chore of feeding the bloodhounds which the sheriff kept behind the jail.

While serving his time, David learned a valuable lesson: when a father breaks the law, the whole family suffers the consequences. As far as I know, he was never again convicted of a crime. Upon his release, David was eager to go to a new state for a fresh start.

Arkansas Bound, 1920

"Land of Opportunity" was a campaign slogan launched to attract new settlers to the sparsely populated state of Arkansas. With high hopes, the Motes family with seven children headed to Arkansas in the spring of 1920. The youngest child at that time, Tom, was less than a year old, and Mary held him on her lap all the way.

Living like gypsies, the Motes family traveled along well-worn roads. The covered wagon which became their home was terribly crowded because it carried everything they owned. It was far too small for the whole family to huddle inside, so the bigger children walked as much as possible.

Sixteen-year-old Annie and fourteen-year-old Jesse were given the responsibility of "driving" or herding the milk cows along behind the wagon. David and Mary made camp late in the afternoon near a small town or community so the mules and cows could rest and graze alongside the road. Where there were homes and people, there was sure to be a steady source of fresh water to sustain them.

It was customary for David and his son Jesse to introduce themselves to the local men and let them know of the Motes family's intentions and destination. If it seemed to be a nice place to spend a few days, David would inquire concerning a job that he could do or a service he could perform. He and his family would welcome a chance to remain camped for a few days.

Walking with God in the Backwoods

When the local citizens were satisfied that the strangers were no threat, they might donate fresh eggs from their laying hens and fresh produce from their vegetable gardens. Many good people had compassion on the Motes family who were traveling with a crying toddler and six other hungry children.

Even when a member of the community seemed harsh and unfriendly, he would let the travelers fill their containers with clean water for drinking and cooking. Reluctantly, he would let David and Jesse water the mules and cows in return for the assurance that the travelers would soon be on their way.

Four-year-old Helen had been riding in the wagon most of the day and was eager to scamper about in search of nearby twigs for the campfire. Eleven-year-old Ellie was assigned to follow her closely to keep her safe. Nine-year-old Levi and seven-year-old William explored farther away and came back dragging larger tree limbs to be cut smaller with an axe and a hatchet. Most days, the boys returned like the biblical shepherds with glad tidings and great joy, for they had discovered a small stream or a shaded creek to splash in.

Mixing corn bread batter, Mary hummed a Gospel song as she prepared to fry griddle cakes in a cast-iron skillet over an open fire. The Motes family often had a meal of hot corn bread and a cup of fresh milk from the cow. Riding all day with a squirming baby on her lap was hard for Mary, but she was determined to enjoy the break from gardening, home canning, cleaning house, making beds, and sweeping floors.

Mary enjoyed camping in the outdoors and seeing the variety of scenery that comes with slow travel.

Some nights, Annie, being so tired she could hardly stand on her feet, would fill a tin pan with water and carry it inside the covered wagon where the baby was sleeping. She would take advantage of the small window of private time for a refreshing sponge bath using a bar of homemade lye soap. Ellie was eager for Annie to take over the care of little Helen so she could have a turn to sponge-bathe. It was quite difficult for Mary and her girls to maintain a sense of dignity under such primitive circumstances. Mary's sponge bath would have to wait until the last glow of the campfire when all the children were washed and sound asleep for the night.

The things that some modern campers do when they are improvising, Mary did on a regular basis. She stripped the dirty shirt from her baby, dipped it into a pan of warm water, rubbed it with lye soap, and used it for a washcloth. When she was finished washing the child, the shirt was wrung out and used to dry him. Both the child and the shirt were clean, and there had been no need of a washcloth or a towel. Homemade lye soap used for bathing was also used for washing the few dishes and for laundry soap. Mary chose not to complain as she took every challenging situation in stride.

The bedding used to cushion their wagon seat while riding was spread inside a tattered canvas tent where the campers would sleep at night. On a hot night, a bedroll could be placed on the freshly grazed grass at the campsite near the tent and smoldering campfire. Like every mother, Mary lay at night making a mental note of the chores to be done tomorrow.

Mary couldn't go very many days without washing diapers. The pee-pee diapers had been hung to dry inside the wagon and reused. Soiled diapers were shook out in the tall grass along the roadside and also hung inside the wagon. The used diapers didn't smell as bad after they were dry. A slightly soiled diaper could sometimes be folded in such a way that allowed for it to be reused. Though this initial problem was solved, the poor baby didn't always smell so sweet.

It would take the Motes family six months to travel three hundred miles from Phil Campbell, Alabama, to Beebe, Arkansas, where David's favorite sister, Kathy Fowler, lived. There would be two more children, James and John Henry, born to David and Mary after their move to Arkansas.

Like other brave settlers who traveled toward unclaimed land in the interior of the United States in the early 1900s, the Motes family was placing their lives at risk. Though doctors sometimes made house calls, they couldn't travel far from town. Many of their patients did not have a telephone to call for a doctor. Hospitals in distant towns were too many miles away for people who relied on mules pulling a wagon as their only source of transportation.

In the event of an illness or injury, it was of great comfort to have someone in the household who could pray a prayer mixed with faith. The person who could "get a hold of God" during a medical emergency was usually the mother. "If I Could Hear My Mother Pray Again" was the title of a popular song that was a favorite in David and Mary's era that captured the essence of a mother's walk with God and spiritual power in prayer.

Mary had known many years in the isolation of the backwoods and was acquainted with loneliness where praying was an act of faith and freedom. She discovered that the spirit of a mere mortal could soar like an eagle and be lifted above the heartaches and hardships of life. It was easier for her as a mother to commune with God while she nursed her infant, darned clothes for her children, and cooked food for her family. As a mother, she was the one who had walked the floors at night with a sick baby because her exhausted husband would have to do harder manual labor the following day. Roles were well defined for poor, uneducated people like David and Mary who grew up knowing what would be expected of them. Mary had no expectation of being relieved of her duties, for hard work and cruel deprivation were as certain for poor people as death and taxes were for all others.

—∿—

Crossing the Mississippi River

The mighty Mississippi River was a magnificent sight for the Motes family. David and Mary were confident that if others had crossed on a ferry boat, they could do it as well. The sight of so much water must have made the heart of the children begin to race as they struggled with a combination of excitement and trepidation.

Blinders were placed on the mules and on the cows to keep them from seeing such a frightening sight, which could cause them to become unmanageable. If the animals could see anything, it was only the ground where they were stepping. They were gently led and coaxed onto the ferry by the same familiar voices that gave commands to them every day of their life. There was such relief for the anxious travelers when they set foot on the other side of the river without incident.

Beebe, Arkansas, 1920

Soon after arriving in Beebe, Arkansas, Annie met James Foster, when he came to visit at her Aunt Kathy's house. He was six years older than Annie and took a great interest in her. James was a nephew to Aunt Kathy's husband. He and Annie exchanged addresses and began writing letters. James ran a general store at Shelbyville that had a small area inside, which was set aside to be used as a post office. He was not only a neighborhood merchant but the local post master. Having tested positive for TB during his tour of duty in World War I, James was considered a disabled veteran. With the money he had saved while in the military, he paid cash ($4,000) for eighty acres of property at Grange with a house, barn, and outbuildings. James had such great wisdom and common sense that other men went to him for financial advice.

James promised Annie that he would come for her soon to whisk her away in his truck so they could be married. Upon arriving, James was directed to the woods where Annie was helping Jesse saw logs for their father who was hewing them into railroad ties. Annie said good-bye to her father and Jesse and went to the house to gather her few belongings. With a tearful good-bye to her mother and younger siblings, Annie left with James. Annie and James produced three children, Argie, Arvis, and Emmer.

With weakened lungs, James succumbed to pneumonia and died in March of 1932, at the age of thirty-four, when his and Annie's first-born child was only six years old. Annie was suddenly a widow with three small children to support. During her time of grief, she needed help from a family member, but Helen was already married to Johnny Smith and Ellie was married to Jesse Smith and had two small children, Mary Jane and Robert, to care for.

Since twenty-one-year-old Levi was very capable in the kitchen and could manage a household, the decision was made that he should go to stay with Annie in her time of great need. While Levi did the housework, the cooking, and taking care of the three little children, Annie ran the grocery store and served as post mistress. Levi used the pickup truck that had belonged to Annie's deceased husband to haul groceries and dry goods from Batesville to the Shelbyville General Store.

During the time that he lived with Annie, Levi met a sixteen-year-old girl that lived across the stream on the adjacent property. As a result of a whirlwind romance, they rushed into a quick marriage. The young girl was added to the household for a short time with Levi, Annie, and the three children. Almost immediately, the unhappy girl realized she had made a terrible mistake. The marriage ended three months later though Levi did not file for divorce for many years.

Annie met a good man and was married again after six months of widowhood. Annie and her new husband, Elvie Cooper, produced a daughter named Vera Mae. The farmwork kept them occupied, and the farm animals kept them tied down because it was necessary to feed them at the end of each day. As hard times came, Annie and Elvie had no automobile and could not easily visit far from home.

Receiving free land in a homestead agreement with the government had been David and Mary's motivation for relocating to Arkansas; however, they found that staying in one place was just too difficult. Soon they were moving about in the northeastern part of Arkansas as opportunities opened up for work.

Annie and her family were left behind by her parents who rarely came to visit. As her brothers and sisters were married and dispersed to distant counties, Annie received occasional information of their whereabouts. She received so few visits from her brothers and sisters that her children hardly knew most of their relatives. Annie was a capable farm wife and homemaker who was a gifted seamstress and made beautiful quilts in her spare time.

Annie had craved stability and security and appreciated having a home of her own. She stated emphatically, "I walked every step of the way, from Alabama to Arkansas." Jesse had also walked, but he didn't talk about it. He probably took a few turns at the reins while his dad walked with the younger children. When the younger children became tired, they were allowed to take a turn riding on the buckboard seat. There was little space for more than a driver and Mary holding the baby, but two small children could be wedged into the seat between them for a short time. It was a long, hard trip for the skinny children who walked much of the way. Rarely did the Motes family talk about their experiences in the past nor did they talk about the future. They lived in the present and only dealt with that which a new day brought to them.

When Annie and Elvie were too old to handle working on the farm, they moved to the small town of Cave City, where Annie experienced widowhood once again. She suffered with breast cancer which resulted in the necessity of having one breast removed. Annie lived a long, productive life and faithfully attended the Baptist church. She died at the age of ninety-three as a result of stomach cancer.

Annie's first born, Argie Sullivan, is my oldest cousin. She is still living in the area of Cave City and turned ninety years old in 2015.

—∿—

Jesse Marries U'Veelia, 1929

David and Mary's oldest son, Jesse, found a wife, U'veelia Wilson, near Saffel where she lived with her family in the Black River bottoms. Jesse found it interesting that he was born in Lawrence County, Alabama, and Veelia was born in Lawrence County, Arkansas. The two were married in 1929, and their first child, Ella Mae was born in November of 1930.

The *U* was dropped from U'Veelia's name, and all who knew and loved her pronounced it "Veelee." She had long dark hair and was one quarter American Indian. She had been told that her unusual name was an Indian word that referred to *rain*. Veelia was very sensitive about her Comanche ancestry. She had personal reasons why she did not want to be identified as an Indian. It is possible that memories remained of a time when Indians suffered horrible discrimination due to their primitive lifestyle and lack of education. Veelia's ancestors had lived with fear of being sent *west* for genocidal removal. Many years would pass before having an American Indian heritage could be celebrated.

Jesse and Veelia had three sets of twins. One set was born in 1932, another set in 1934, and the third set was born in

1936. Each set of twins was a girl and a boy. Veelia gave birth to seven children within a period of six years. Due to the fact that Jesse and Veelia had several multiple births, they were informed that they qualified for government assistance, but they chose not to pursue the possibility. As time went on, Jesse and Veelia had a total of fourteen children as they moved from place to place in the northeastern part of Arkansas. They enjoyed much the same unsettled lifestyle that David and Mary lived and often moved along with them to a new location. Veelia liked her mother-in-law, and the two families did well together. Jesse and his boys were also farm laborers or worked in the timber industry at sawmills while Veelia and the girls chopped cotton and picked cotton as Mary had done.

When Jesse and Veelia reached retirement age, they settled in Stone County near Mountain View, where they and their grown children built a nondenominational Pentecostal church on their property, which included a family cemetery in the church yard. Many of Jesse and Veelia's children became ministers of the Gospel of Jesus Christ. After many years of suffering from diabetes, Jesse died at the age of eighty-six, leaving Veelia a widow after sixty-three years of marriage.

Toward the end of the 1900s, people of American Indian ancestry were encouraged to register and receive a degree of compensation from the government. Veelia would have no part of that. Even in old age, she remained uncomfortable with the idea of registering with a government agency for being part Indian. Veelia lived to be ninety-one years old and faithfully attended her family's church where she stationed herself nearest the podium in a rocking chair so she could hear everything and wouldn't miss anything.

The One-Room School

It was a privilege to go to school and to become educated. Sometimes, the Motes boys were kept from school during part of the term to work beside their dad. It was necessary that they share the burden of making a living for the family. If David and Mary's children didn't have clothes fit to wear to school, they might not bother to go at all.

Children from transient families suffered a tremendous disadvantage. They often felt inferior to students who were younger, more advanced in their education, and better established socially. Even when Levi was too sick to do manual labor, he assisted his mother by sitting at home with the babies. Levi dropped out of school having achieved a second-grade education.

When the Motes children did attend school, it was most often a small one-room school in the country that only went through the eighth grade. It was heated by a wood-burning stove, which the older boys helped to tend during the day. Being without modern plumbing, there was an outdoor toilet built in the backyard. Some schools had the luxury of two

Mabel Margaret Motes Bufford

toilets placed at opposite sides of the yard—one designated for boys and one for the girls.

Public school teachers often had a higher degree of education and refinement than others in the community where they served. Being a school teacher was not just a job or even a career, it was considered by many to be a sacred calling. Most often, the teacher was a prim and proper single lady and was highly respected by the parents as well as her students. A great amount of self-discipline was required for a teacher to achieve such an exalted position. The students responded to their teacher with "Yes, ma'am" or "No, ma'am," for they were taught to be polite and to address all ladies in such a manner.

Most often, there was one schoolteacher responsible for the education of twenty to thirty students from first grade through the eighth grade. It was necessary that each group of students stay quiet and busy with their book work while the teacher worked with another group. Under those circumstances, the teacher had to be a stern disciplinarian. It was helpful when two older siblings kept their younger brother or sister wedged between them on the bench seat to keep them "corralled." Occasionally, a teacher had to administer a paddling to an unruly little rascal as a last resort. Any problem the teacher had with a student was reported to the parents who administered additional discipline. The fact that children were disciplined and taught proper behavior at home made it possible for the schoolteacher to maintain order in the schoolhouse.

—⚬⚬—

The Olden Days

In a group setting, fathers "in the olden days" often entertained the children with tales of having been "taken to the woodshed" as youngsters. Like veterans exchanging war stories, the man with the best story was as proud as a soldier with a badge of honor. Though the stories were funny and the children laughed, it "put the fear of God" into unruly children who misbehaved.

—⚬⚬—

Parenting Style and Discipline

When Levi was seventeen, he was so sick he feared that he would not live to be twenty-one. In an effort to comfort him, Mary told Levi an encouraging story. She said once when he was a baby, he became very sick and she feared that he might die. A circuit riding preacher came by their house, and she asked him to pray for baby Levi. After the preacher finished his prayer, he told Mary that her sick baby would not die. He would live to be an old man and see the end time. It was assumed that he would probably go to be with the Lord in the rapture. Armed with this information, faith arose in Levi's heart as he began to recover, and it gave him a sense of being invincible. He didn't think about it often throughout his life, but it did embolden him anytime he faced a life-threatening situation.

Mary insisted that her children never say anything bad about anyone. "If you can't say something good, don't say anything at all," she instructed. Her children learned the lesson well. Each one gave little information which could be passed down for future generations concerning their childhood. I suppose it was because there was so little good to tell.

The advice David practiced and passed down was, "Keep your children busy with manual labor." He taught his sons to make cross ties and axe handles to sell and passed along his skills as a farmer and a hunter. He gave his children lessons in singing and reading shape notes, but none shared his love and passion for it. Years later, he would try to teach his grandchildren, but most of them dreaded the lessons and endured the experience.

David and Mary sharecropped for a few years on the "Prader place" near Flag Slough, in Poinsett County, where they raised cotton. David and the boys used an implement called a single-tree pulled by a team of mules. The single-tree looked like a garden plow with wooden handles for guiding it as one walked behind. During the winter months, David taught the boys to trap animals, dry the skins, and prepare the fur to sell. David told his children repeatedly, "You can *stay out* of trouble a lot easier than you can *get out* of trouble."

In the culture of David and Mary's time, corporal punishment of children was common. Most toddlers were spanked soundly and taught to be submissive to authority. A good spanking was one severe enough to stop the bad behavior. In that day, spanking a child so lightly that they required frequent spanking was considered inadequate discipline. The most questionable advice David received and passed along was, "If you don't whip your children when they are young, they will whip you when they get older." Mary preferred to be the disciplinarian for her small children to spare them from a severe thrashing by their father who had a tendency toward being too harsh. The young Motes children were not accustomed to having large amounts of parental affection. In David and Mary's situation, work and chores were the higher priority in life.

Loss of a Mother

While living near Flag Slough, David taught singing by notes at both the Cooper and Hanes Baptist church and at the Long Creek Baptist church. Though he was getting to do what he enjoyed most, there was little or no pay for it. Farming was such hard work, and they were always looking for an easier way to make a living. The Motes family chose to move away.

David and Mary seemed to prefer living in woodsy mountains, which reminded them of Alabama, but there were less job opportunities there. David got a job piloting a ferry across Black River near Saffell during the Depression. It didn't pay enough, considering that it kept a family "tied down." With several young men in the family, there was the opportunity to teach each one how to do the job and let them take turns.

As Christmas day arrived, Mary was gravely ill and suffered discomfort in her chest. In addition to the fear of dying, she was deeply concerned for the well-being of her young children if they should have to grow up without her. Mary was aware that the apostle Paul referred to believers as *saints* in the New Testament. Being a woman of prayer, she would have taken note that the prayers of saints are kept in heaven in golden vials like perfume, according to Revelations 5:8. In that atmosphere, her prayers would not become stale with age or grow old and expire. Having great faith in God, she prayed continually until she got assurance that her children would be all right.

When Mary experienced pain with each breath, she knew death was eminent. As she lay in bed on the day after Christmas, there was a knock at the door. One of the children answered the door and announced to their father, "Someone needs a ride across the river."

Mary tugged at David's arm, and he bent over to hear what she wanted to say to him. Struggling to breathe, she whispered, "Have Levi to go. I can't die with him in the room." When Levi returned from the river, he found that his mother

Walking with God in the Backwoods

had passed away. On December 26, 1933, Mary Ursley Motes died of pneumonia at the age of forty-nine. She left behind several minor children with the youngest, John Henry, being only eight years old. Levi was the oldest of Mary's children still living in the home.

Levi sewed a shift-style dress for his mother's burial using black fabric while David built a wooden coffin. The next day, they loaded the coffin on the wagon to be pulled by mules to the Ward Cemetery at Saffell where other family members and friends had prepared an open grave. The water was extremely high in the Black River bottoms as the wagon was pulled through a muddy slough. The mules struggled as the water came up to their belly and into the wagon. Yelling at the mules and hitting them on the rump with the end of the reigns, David forced them onward while his children riding in the wagon lifted the coffin to keep it from getting wet.

Bewildered over the loss of his wife, the grieving Mr. Motes found it difficult to cope with his parental responsibilities. He saw no reward as a result of Mary diligently seeking the Lord. Hard work and deprivation were all she had known in her short life. He didn't see that it had done any good to pray. It was as if the wind had been taken out of his sails—he began to lie around more and work less. As a result of his faith being shaken, he became short with all his children and physically abusive.

As a young man of twenty-two, Levi needed to leave the family home to earn money for supporting his minor siblings.

William, being a teenager, was old enough to help his father with cooking meals and doing chores and housework. The three youngest boys, Tom, Jim, and John Henry, were taken to live with Jesse and Veelia who had a growing family of their own. Though David couldn't see it, Mary's prayers were being answered. Long before Mary's death, God had chosen to bless Veelia with the gift of mothering, and she became a beloved mother figure to the grieving children. Veelia's assistance was invaluable in maintaining a calm and stable environment while other family members worked outside the home. Mary's death did not hinder God from granting the desires of her heart.

> As one whom his mother comforteth, so will I comfort
> you; and ye shall be comforted...
>
> —Isaiah 66:13

Amazing Grace

DEPLETED AND DIMINISHED BY THE worldwide flu epidemic of 1918, two world wars, a great depression, droughts, and the dust storms that had blown away much of the topsoil in the south central United States, many Americans had been brought to their knees. It had been a time of trouble and in such a dimension they had not envisioned: the infamous attack on Pearl Harbor had shaken their sense of security, the unspeakable atrocities of Hitler's Third Reich shocked their sense of humanity, and our use of the first atomic bomb numbed the confidence in our own morality. With the resolve that this situation should never be permitted to develop again, measures were taken toward world government with the creation of the World Bank in 1944 and the signing of the charter for the United Nations in 1945.

During periods of bewilderment, some Christians had wondered if Hitler could be the *Anti-Christ* and if the world was approaching the end of time and the day of the Lord's return. In their distress, many Christian parents and grandparents cried out to God for their country and for the future of their children. It might have been that God responded with a visitation of the Holy Spirit. Many mighty miracles were reported as people lined up at special meetings and tent revivals to receive prayer from men and women who possessed a greater measure of faith.

In 1945, the rumbling war machinery of World War II had come to a laborious halt, allowing the victorious American soldiers to begin returning home. They were greeted by jubilant crowds in our grateful nation and with the comforting embrace of relieved and thankful families. The more fortunate soldiers returned to adoring sweethearts or to loving wives. Some returned to family-owned businesses and farms in the South where there was a respect for higher education, faithful church attendance, and noble family values. This valiant generation of Americans ushered in what we now know as the baby boom generation, of which I am a member.

The Bachelors

Levi and his aging father bought forty acres of wooded land in a sparsely populated area of the Ozarks around 1940. The terrain was so rough with rocks and boulders that a nice car should not be driven there. Their property was reached by truck or by a wagon pulled by mules, but they didn't always have an automobile or even a mule. They were most often limited to walking and hitchhiking everywhere they went. Though they lived in poverty and isolation, they were pleased to be landowners eighteen miles from Mountain View, Arkansas.

Levi and Mr. Motes incorporated friends and family to help dig a well about eighteen feet deep and lined the inside with rocks. Outside the well, rocks were placed waist high so no person or animal would fall into it. A structure consisting of a frame with a roof overhead kept the leaves and trash from blowing into the water. The frame gave support for a pulley that hung above the well. A rope was tied securely to the rafter with a bucket dangling from the other end. The bucket was dropped into the well and retrieved by pulling the rope as it traveled over the pulley for "drawing water."

Enough land was cleared for Levi and his father to build the two-room log cabin which they shared. It was a primitive home having only a living room and a small kitchen. The kitchen had an old wood-burning "cook stove" with an oven. The cane-bottom chairs that went with the homemade kitchen table were carried to the living room/bedroom to provide seating when company came.

In the summer months, the doors were often allowed to stand wide open to let in the light and the breeze. There was no screen door to hinder the dog, which wandered in at will, and so did the insects. Mr. Motes sprinkled salt liberally on the mattress in an effort to eliminate the pesky bedbugs and to discourage poisonous spiders that bite.

A wood-burning stove occupied the center of the room between two beds which were placed against the outside walls. Black tar paper covered the walls inside the cabin to keep the howling winter wind at bay. The house was pitch-black on a moonless night and dimly lit during the day, for the windows were too small to let an adequate amount of light inside.

Walking with God in the Backwoods

Without a barn for storage, it was necessary for Levi and Mr. Motes to build a small lean-to on the far side of the house. Dry firewood and a garden plow were placed inside to be protected from the rain. With nails driven into the outer walls, space was utilized for hanging the crosscut saw and small hand tools. Dangling from a nail nearest to the door was a harness kept within arm's reach for the mule.

Batchin' was a term Levi used to describe the living arrangement for single men who did not have the benefit of a woman in the house. He and his dad didn't have much and didn't need much. The small cabin was sufficient for the two men who preferred to be outdoors. Levi had a positive outlook on life and did not complain or murmur about anything.

There were very few ways to earn money in Stone County, but one of them was to dig the roots of the Black Haw tree and peel the bark off the roots. After drying the bark, it could be sold for forty-two cents a pound and shipped to St. Louis for its medical benefits. They were told that the root bark was being processed to make medicine for the World War II soldiers who had venereal disease.

Levi hitchhiked to other counties in search of work where strangers frequently asked him, "Whar ye from?"

"Stone County," Levi replied proudly, as if telling the name of his hometown. The strangers responded knowingly as if they could picture the exact location. Counties were more significant in those days when small towns were little more than a community and totally unfamiliar to people a few miles away. In those days, important business transactions took place at the county seat, which was usually a large town that seemed far away.

Living like a tortured prisoner in isolation, arthritic pain forced Mr. Motes to stay indoors for days during cold and rainy weather. He heated cloth bags of salt which he placed on his aching joints. Lying under the covers, he stared at the red glow in the wood burner, hour after hour, as he waited for sleep to overtake him. He thought of Mary and how much he missed her. Without children to tend in their old age, she could have worked less and enjoyed life a little more. He could not—nor would he—consider replacing Mary. She had been a good woman, a good wife, a good mother, and a good Christian. He was comforted by the knowledge that she had gone to her reward in heaven, but he was confused by the absence of rewards for the righteous here on earth. In childhood, Mary had known much sadness, and in her adult life, there were hardships in abundance. In his misery, Mr. Motes wondered, *Is this all there is to life—work hard and die?* He could see no rewards on earth for Mary being a righteous person and praying fervently. With no one around to be the recipient of his anger, he lashed out at God and sank deeper into depression. Realizing that he was becoming a bitter old man, Mr. Motes tried to redirect his focus. He wondered if he had made a dreadful mistake in moving his family to

Arkansas where neither he nor his grown sons had found prosperity in this *land of opportunity*.

Goat Farming

Mr. Motes and Levi raised goats which produced milk to provide for their need and to sell in the community. Some people with stomach disorders thought milk from a goat was better for their health and tasted better than milk from a cow. Occasionally, a neighbor arranged to buy goat's milk for a cranky newborn baby with colic or frequent vomiting. This was the remedy most widely accepted before infant formula was available.

A small shed was built to house the goats at night and provide shelter for them during bad weather. Goats were a poor man's choice because they were less expensive to feed than cows. Cows required a better quality of pasture land, but goats would eat anything green, including briars. The goat lot could be moved when the area was made totally barren. In this way, large areas were cleared of underbrush and vegetation. With less vegetation near the house, there was less of a problem with ticks and chiggers.

Times were hard during the Great Depression and just as hard during the extreme drought that came soon afterward. With less money in circulation, the process of obtaining goods was done by bartering or trading. Trading was so common

Mabel Margaret Motes Bufford

that the word was used instead of *shopping*. Levi might point out a country store and say, "Thet's whar I do my tradin'."

Annie's daughter Argie tells of their family having a four-acre patch of peas on a hillside near Grange. "We had to pick the whole patch just to get enough peas for one meal," she said.

When the economy began to recover in other areas of the nation, Arkansas remained a depressed state for lack of industry. Raising chickens in long chicken houses would eventually become a reliable source of income for ambitious families who stayed in the mountains close to White River.

—∞—

Personality Plus

As an adult, Levi was a mere five feet and four inches and his younger brother, William, towered over him. Levi was very skinny, weighing a mere 125 pounds. He was a good man, both tough and tender. He smiled easily and laughed frequently for he genuinely loved people. In his mind's eye, he could work the hardest, lift the most weight, and whoop any man. What Levi lacked in size, he made up in confidence.

A few people dismissed Levi as a braggart, but most people were amused by his big talk and colorful exaggeration. He was such a likeable guy that he had little occasion to fight; he managed to disarm irate people and neutralize volatile situations with his quick wit. In those days, being honorable was very important to most men. Levi knew there could be no honor for anyone who beats up a little man. Even worse dishonor would come to that one who is beaten by a little man.

Levi was an entertainer at heart and possessed a natural talent for comic timing. His storytelling abilities were most appreciated by lonely men who were starved for diversion and entertainment. Levi had no interest in talking about sports and politics or arguing about religion. He was careful to never talk about the faults and failures of other people. That didn't leave him a lot to talk about except farming, gardening, and the weather. It was near impossible to entertain others with those topics. Most often, Levi told stories about animals and hunting. He especially enjoyed telling stories about bears. The style of his storytelling was similar to that of Jerry Clower, a country comedian from Mississippi. Levi probably never heard of the man, but you would think they were raised together. Like a comedian, Levi could embellish a story for the sake of amusement and still be respected as an honest man.

—✄—

Working on the River

For a short time, Levi took a job shelling on White River where he lived on a house boat which housed temporary workers. Diving in shallow areas to the bottom of the muddy river, he and other young men felt around for the muscle shells that had accumulated there. One of the young men suggested they tie their pants legs at the ankles and slip the muscle shells into their denim overalls. They could then come ashore and empty their pants leg rather than making so many trips to the riverbank. It worked fine until a coworker having his pants legs full of shells stepped into a hole and could not get out. The weight held him under, and he drowned before anyone was aware that he was in trouble. After that tragedy, Levi employed another method. He tied a rope from a rowboat to his waist and piled all the muscle shells directly into the boat which floated behind him.

Fatalities as a result of drowning were not the only concern for those who worked in the river. Experiencing a high incidence of carbuncles or painful boils, the men risked blood poisoning from working in nasty water. Levi tried to stay near the sandbar where there was less danger and less filthy muck and mire.

Muscle shells from the riverbed were sold to a business in the thriving town of Newport where they were used to make buttons. Some of the shells were shipped overseas. When the button factory went out of business, a mountain of shells remained. Some people took the white shells to cover the graves of their loved ones. Not only were the white shells decorative, but they kept the grave site from becoming obscure in the grass and weeds.

Working in the Timber

For many of his bachelor years, Levi worked at far away sawmills in various counties in the northeastern section of the state of Arkansas. When the supply of timber was exhausted in one area, the mill was dismantled and moved to another location to harvest a fresh "stand of timber." The saw motor was like a noisy generator; in addition, there was a deafening, high-pitched sound produced as the blade cut through the logs. Damage to the hearing was one of the perils of the job that affected Levi and many of his coworkers.

Traveling far from home, Levi made his bed wherever he could. He traveled with very little in the way of personal belongings. At new or temporary work sites, there were no cabins built for the men. A lean-to made with canvas tarps tied between trees provided shelter for the workers from the rain or the dew. Sometimes, the men would sleep in an empty box car that was attached to a parked logging train. One time, Levi rode the train along with some friendly hobos just for the thrill of it. When they neared the Rocky Mountains, he decided he didn't want to go any further and hitched a ride on another train that was heading back. Levi led a diverse life, trying one new job after another. Hitchhiking from one location to the next was easy since men driving alone were often eager to have conversation with someone new. Everyone had an adventurous story to tell although their exploits were often exaggerated.

A toothbrush and toothpaste were seldom seen among the rugged young woodsmen who followed the sawmill and logging industry. They tended to their dental hygiene in their own way. A twig cut from a black gum tree made an ideal toothpick. When the end of the toothpick was soft and frayed, they used it to clean the plaque off their teeth. If a tooth needed to be pulled, it was often done by a friend with a pair of wire pliers. Most of the men chewed tobacco and perfected the art of spitting long distances. In the event of a bee sting or a snake bite, a wad of chewing tobacco, taken directly from the mouth, was placed on the affected area for medicine.

Sharecropping in the Bottoms, 1946

The miles of low farmland in the north eastern portion of Arkansas were referred to as the "bottoms." In the spring, the farmers prepared their fields for planting, and there would be cotton to chop. In the fall at harvest time, workers were needed to pick the fluffy white cotton. Levi hitched a ride to the farming community between Grubbs and Weiner to search for a temporary job and watched for the possibility of land to rent in the following spring.

In 1946, Levi persuaded his father to partner with him to sharecrop near the Flag Slough ditch. Levi had nothing but a willingness to work while his father had acquired a team of mules and a wagon. They arranged to borrow $400 from

Buck Hurley at the Newport Cotton Gin for the purpose of putting in a small crop of cotton. Twenty acres was about all one man could handle without a farm tractor. While picking cotton, Levi met Eva West, a thirty-four-year-old single mother, and Mike, her nine-year-old son.

Eva and her son were new to the community near Weiner, having just moved from the family farm near Grubbs. Eva's aging father, Sam West, had purchased a forty-acre farm which had two old shacks pulled together to make one house. Eva cooked, cleaned, and cared for her ailing father who suffered from asthma. Eva's mother, Della, stayed behind to manage the farm near Grubbs where she cared for two retarded sons who were middle age and capable of doing yard and garden work. While Eva's older sisters chose to live in faraway cities, Eva remained with her parents and younger sister, Mabel, for she needed their help in the upbringing of her son, Mike.

Levi Marries Eva, 1947

It was a time when a man's worth was determined by how hard he worked; in that aspect, Levi was quite impressive. While picking cotton near Levi, Eva found the thirty-six-year-old bachelor fascinating and refreshing. She enjoyed his colorful stories, and he was pleased to entertain her. Like those who knew her best, he called her "Evie." As the days

Mabel Margaret Motes Bufford

went by, they talked of more serious things while they worked side by side. Eva wondered if he would stay after the harvest; her future depended on the decision he would make.

Eva had dreamed of having a large family, and she feared that time was running out for her. Having a family sounded mighty fine to Levi too. Eva was the first woman he had found who gave him reason to hope for a family and a better life. Levi was suddenly motivated to fix the mistake he'd made fifteen years before when he had married a young girl. Using some of the money he'd earned from picking cotton, he filed for a divorce and began the stressful wait for the final papers to come in the mail.

In an agreement with his father, Levi gave up all interest in the property they had shared in the mountains of Stone County in exchange for the team of mules, wagon and plow, and a bale of cotton still in the field. Levi chose to stay in the bottoms that winter with the intention of helping Mr. West by sharecropping with him the following year.

It was a bitter cold day, February 2, 1947, when Levi and Eva with Mike in tow walked a mile to the home of a justice of the peace where they could be married. Eva was destined to become Levi's wife and the mother of six more children. With winter in full swing, it was the wrong time of year for a good start in a new life. Fortunately, Mr. West was willing to share his shabby house, which provided them a much-needed sense of security.

The Overnight Guest

Levi had Eva's help to write personal letters to his father rather than sending verbal messages by way of friends and relatives who traveled back and forth between the mountains and the bottoms. Hitching a ride, Mr. Motes came to visit Levi and other family members who lived nearby. He could not stay in the bottoms long because a neighbor had been asked to check on his mule, Ole Jenny, and the watchdog.

Mr. Motes was invited to share Mike's full-sized bed for the overnight stay. Mike remembers taking the far side of the bed and rolling toward the wall to allow the old man to sleep on the edge. A surprise for Mike came in the darkness when Mr. Motes leaned over him and spat a mouthful of tobacco on the wall. Droplets of tobacco juice splattered off the wall and onto Mike's face; he would never forget that experience. In the future, an empty tin can would be provided as a "spit can" to guests who chewed tobacco.

Mr. Motes was eager to get back to the cabin which he and Levi affectionately called the "tin-top." He fared well in his crude lifestyle for he was now accustomed to being alone and occupied himself in his old age by growing tobacco plants for his own use. Little of his effort was required to cultivate the stony ground in the springtime, for he would plant seeds in a barren spot where a brush pile had been burned the year before.

At the end of the harvest season, when the newlyweds gathered the fruit of their labor, there was the added blessing of a baby girl—Levi's first child and Eva's first daughter. Audrey Della Motes was born October 25, 1947.

> Whoso findeth a wife findeth a good thing, and
> obtaineth favor of the Lord.

—Proverbs 18:22

A New Name in Glory
1948

Putting down roots came very hard for most of David and Mary's children and for many of their grandchildren. Few could claim a hometown as they grew up, and they wearied of always being the new student at school. The closest some came to finding a place to settle was the Long Creek community. The younger sons found wives among the families who lived in that area long before Levi met Eva. A comforting sense of community could not make up for the fact they could hardly make a living there.

While Ellie's family lived nearby, her young husband, Jesse Smith, died of pneumonia after working in a misty rain. Though he was uneducated, he was a very good man and the love of Ellie's life. He had been a dear friend to Levi, and his passing caused great sorrow. Levi designed a small tombstone marking his gravesite at the Clark Cemetery by placing a few marbles in wet cement.

Ellie needed a husband to help her to survive during a difficult time with two small children. She was soon married again to Matt Jordan, who was a religious man and apt to preach when he talked to others about Bible scriptures. She surprised her family members by referring to her new husband respectfully as Mr. Jordan.

Several of Levi's relatives, his brothers Jesse and Tom and their sister Ellie, moved their families to an area which they called the East Bottoms. It was a cotton-farming area near Truman in a community called Weona.

Levi thoroughly enjoyed his extended family, and feeling a great sense of loyalty, he desired to move with them. He was not accustomed to staying long in one place. While Levi had been a bachelor, he could come and go as he pleased, made spontaneous decisions, and was openhanded when he had money. Being the head of a growing family made those traits less desirable. Levi and Eva took Mike and baby Audrey and moved to Weona, where they sharecropped in 1948 for one growing season.

Becoming a sharecropper was an easy choice for returning soldiers like Tom who had recently left fighting in Europe during World War II. They could show up without anything and arrange a partnership with someone who owned a team of mules, a plow and planter, or tractor with necessary equipment. A sharecropper had to ask for a loan in the springtime for money to live on and to buy seeds for planting with the intention of paying it back at harvest time. Arrangements for a loan could be made with a government agency or sometimes with the owner of a cotton gin. When the harvest was sold, half of the profit from the crop went to the landowner who had provided primitive housing. For the sharecropper who did not own any farm equipment, he might split his half of the income with the partner who provided the mules or tractor and equipment. Out of their portion, the sharecroppers paid back the money they had borrowed for seed at planting time. Sharecropping did not always raise hardworking farmers above the poverty level, but it gave them enough money to purchase basic grocery items and necessities for survival.

The Pentecostal Experience

While living in the East Bottoms, Levi, Eva, and the children attended a Pentecostal church with all the relatives who had gone there to work. In that small church at Weona Junction, they felt the convicting power of the Holy Spirit which drew them to salvation through Jesus Christ. They were relieved to have their names recorded in the Book of Life in heaven. In the year 1948, their lives were changed and the lives of the whole Motes family would be influenced for future generations.

Mary's daughter, Ellie, and her three daughters-in-law made up a diverse group of ladies: Ellie was mostly Irish, Veelia was part Indian, Elizabeth (Tom's wife) was half German, and Eva was English. After being introduced to a Pentecostal move of the Holy Spirit, all would influence their children for Christ. Though many years had passed since her death, another prayer that Mary had prayed for her children was being answered. I know this to be true, for it is the desire of every believing mother that her children come to the knowledge of Christ. Several of Mary's children and grandchildren have been active in their local churches and some have been called to preach the Gospel of Jesus Christ.

While several of the Motes family members were unified in one mind and one accord, there was an outpouring of the Holy Spirit. Eva had a spiritual experience called the Baptism in the Holy Ghost, which made a profound impact on her. It was somewhat like the New Testament Church had experienced. Levi's salvation experience was less emotional, but it initiated a change that would manifest gradually. Levi and Eva did not suddenly become perfect, but their sins were forgiven. Their personalities were not changed, but their desires were changed to that of righteous desires for right living. Their character was not totally and immediately changed, but a lifelong partnership with God provided daily assistance in combating their weaknesses, faults, and flaws.

Walking with God in the Backwoods

Like healing and growth, Levi and Eva made continual progress toward Christ-like character.

Mary's life had been one of poverty and suffering, and there had been no outward evidence that God was a *rewarder* of her efforts to diligently seek Him. Though Mary did not live to see it, her Heavenly Father had promised to give her the desires of her heart, and He was doing just that. While *wants* are often for material things, *desires* come from the depths of the heart and are often noble. Like baking yeast added to the flour, the experience of Pentecost was added to the Motes family heritage. It appears that spiritual seeds planted by those in one generation can bring forth a harvest in the next generation.

Many of the family members who did not move to Weona were influenced by those who did. Eventually, William moved to Indiana, while Jim and John Henry moved their families to Chicago, where their sister Helen was living with her husband. John Henry and his family of nine children attended a Pentecostal church in Chicago.

A desire for righteousness does not run in a family by accident but by direct intervention of God Almighty. Though God is not willing that anyone should perish, He partners with believing people who pray for others and believe for their salvation. It may be that God does nothing major in our families except in response to prayers.

Israel in the News

For all Christians who had studied biblical prophesies, a radio broadcast concerning Israel was of great interest. They believed Israel was the time piece which would alert believers to God's program. On May 15, 1948, Israel became a nation again for the first time since Jerusalem was attacked by the Romans and the temple was destroyed in 70 AD. The Jewish people being dispersed all over the world and then returning to their homeland to become a nation had been prophesied for the end time—preceding the coming of the Messiah, Jesus Christ. News that Israel had become a nation was like an alarm being sounded as ministers proclaimed, "People, get ready! The Lord is coming back to earth again!" According to Bible prophesy, the generation in existence when this event happens will not all pass away before the end comes (see Luke 21:32).

With the hope of Christ's impending return, ministers encouraged the saints to seek holiness and to be in a constant state of readiness to leave this world. The "holiness movement" which swept the South was a new concept for some of the Motes relatives, especially for Eva. Eva's family roots had been in the Church of Christ at Hankins, which was a convenient walking distance from her childhood home before the church was moved to Grubbs. All the other Motes family members had a history in the Baptist church.

Walking with God in the Backwoods

Hunger and Hardship

When the harvest was completed in Weona, Levi chose to move back to Mr. West's land. Mr. West's health was failing, and he would not live much longer. Eva was relieved to be back with her family and in familiar surroundings to give birth to her third child (me).

There was very little money left after Levi had bought an old truck to haul their few belongings, and it would be a long time until another cotton harvest.

Unfortunately, Levi was not a good money manager; the money he had just got away from him. However, it was customary that husbands had the privilege, as the sole breadwinner, to make all monetary decisions. Soon afterwards, the engine of the truck refused to start and they were isolated in the backwoods. Levi had neglected to stock up on groceries, and that left the family ill prepared for winter. It was a bleak and miserable time on the farm near Weiner. My older brother, Mike, who was eleven years old at the time, remembers those days with sadness.

"A quart jar of peaches was the only food in the house on the day you were born," Mike informed me, "and Grandma West had given that to us." When I questioned him further about it, he told me there were a couple cans of condensed milk also. His mother had been in labor all morning, and there was nothing freshly cooked and nothing left over to eat from the day before. With anxiety building, Mike had cared for Audrey who was a fifteen-month-old toddler. He was cast into a painful moral dilemma as he considered the jar of peaches. Mike dared not take enough of the only jar of peaches to satisfy his own hunger. He dutifully cut some of the peaches with a fork for feeding the baby and then prepared a glass bottle of milk for her. I didn't ask if he took any of the peaches for himself. I suspect that he did not. The incident had made such a painful memory for him that I could not bear to make him relive it just to satisfy my curiosity. I imagine that Mike triumphed over the temptation to fill his empty stomach. That decision would have allowed the torment of hunger to subside, allowing him to think of other pressing issues.

The only information I got concerning my birth was what my mother volunteered. As Mama recalled, she had gone into hard labor before noon while my father was working in the woods nearby. Levi spent most of the daylight hours outdoors even during the winter months. He was an energetic man who busied himself making axe handles and cross ties to sell for income, or cutting firewood to heat the house. Eva told Mike to "bun'el up" as he left to fetch Levi, who was working a short distance from the house. Having determined that birth was imminent, Levi told Mike to summon a neighbor lady. The nearest family lived more than a mile through the woods.

Walking with God in the Backwoods

Delivering a baby could be bloody, messy, and unpleasant; not everyone desired to be involved in such an experience. An in-home delivery by an inexperienced person was more stressful due to the element of danger which could require life-and-death decisions when there was no way to get to the hospital.

With cheeks red from the winter cold, Mike arrived at the neighbor's house by foot, while the lady of the house was placing a meal on the table for her family. The timing of this request for her assistance was inconvenient. Knowing that labor could require long hours of waiting, her husband suggested that she take time to eat before leaving. Invited inside the neighbor's toasty-warm living room, Mike appreciated the chance to warm his hands near the wood-burning stove. Smelling the aroma of hot food was like torture when he was so hungry. Feeling ill at ease, Mike waited patiently while the neighbors enjoyed their meal. He had hoped they would invite him to come to the table, but they did not.

An hour had passed when Mike returned on foot with the reluctant neighbor and her youngest son. Mike was pleased to be with the boy who was his good friend from school. As they neared the house, Mike and his friend were told to run along and play. The neighbor knocked on the door and cautiously opened it as she listened for voices. She was not sure what to expect. "Come right in," Levi said as she entered. "We got us another girl." Levi had tied and cut the umbilical cord and was cleaning up. He was quite a capable man in the type of things one needs to do on the frontier.

Levi began to tell the neighbor lady how the cord had been wrapped around the baby's neck and she was blue at birth. As they examined the new arrival, the only thing that caused them concern was an area on the forehead that remained blue.

While the adults were occupied inside the house, the boys slipped away unnoticed. Mike and his friend had spied some ice nearby that had frozen on the overflow waters; with a good running start, they could skate a long way. When the boys crashed through the ice, they were delighted to find that the receding water had left a thin layer of ice six inches above the ground with no water below. Stamping with their feet they went about deliberately crushing the ice. Mike was pleased to leave the adult concerns to the adults while he and his friend enjoyed just being boys.

"It's a healthy little girl," the neighbor reported to Mike as she summoned her son for the walk back home. With a quick good-bye to his friend, Mike rushed to the house. He took a quick look to find his mother lying in the bed with a tiny baby cradled in one arm. Though weak and pale, Eva greeted him with a broad smile and eagerly showed Mike his new baby sister. Mike looked at the tiny creature that had caused all the fuss. He felt nothing but relief; the crisis was over. There was new life in the dead of winter — and all was well.

Rabbit Trapping

The backwoodsmen often earned money by hunting and trapping wild animals and selling the fur. With many of the predators eliminated, wild rabbits were plentiful. This was God's provision to satisfy the hunger of many poor people during that time in history.

As a child, Mike discovered that a gun with bullets was not necessary for hunting rabbits. Mike had learned from Levi how to trap rabbits in a "rabbit gum." The live trap was made from a portion of hollow log that had been sawed off at the length of about thirty inches. No bait was necessary because rabbits made use of hollow logs instinctively for shelter to escape the winter cold and as a safe place to hide from predators. The back end of the trap was blocked by having a piece of bark or a scrap of a board nailed onto it. This created an inexpensive animal cage. Though it was in a cylinder shape, it was similar to a rural-type mailbox except the trap door placed on the front opened upward rather than downward. A stick was placed inside the trap through a hole that had been drilled in the top of the box toward the back. The stick had been notched about halfway down so it would stay in place until the rabbit entered the trap and pushed it from its position. Another stick was tied to the notched stick and extended above the surface of the box to the trap door at the front. A notch in that stick held the trap door open. Like a mousetrap, the rabbit tripped the notched stick when it went inside which flew upward and caused the trap door to be dropped downward; the unsuspecting rabbit was not harmed but napped in comfort while trapped inside.

Mike checked his rabbit gum every day, knowing that the rabbit he caught would have to be killed for the meat. With the rabbit being a docile creature, it seldom scratched or tried to bite him. Mike gave a hard blow to the back of the rabbit's head with a wooden club just as he had been instructed, and it proved to be a quick and humane death.

The death of an animal was a harsh reality for Mike but unavoidable in obtaining meat. Hunger and poverty enabled Mike to handle the gruesome procedure that was necessary when obtaining meat for his family's meals. He didn't have the strength to skin a rabbit easily when alone, so he waited for his stepfather, Levi, to help him. If skinning the rabbit was not done correctly, the hairs from the rabbit fur would stick to the meat and take greater effort to wash clean. Meat from an old and tough rabbit could be boiled and cooked with dumplings or it could be picked off the bone for rabbit chili. The meat from a young tender rabbit was rolled in flour, seasoned with salt and pepper, and fried in lard. Fried rabbit meat was tasty and had a flavor similar to that of fried chicken. Mike said he was often hungry and did what had to be done out of necessity. Though God provided the meat for the meals, He did not eliminate the struggle and the process. Though butchering an animal had always been an accepted fact of life, modern children are spared seeing the ghastly process.

Eva, Levi, and Mike looked forward to spring weather and planting vegetable seeds in the garden and buying a baby pig to be butchered for meat in the fall. While desiring a sense of security for her children and herself, Eva encouraged Levi to put down roots. I credit her for being a stabilizing influence in his life, for it was she who made a difference.

Managing Poverty

Though they would often depend on the kindness of Eva's family for financial assistance, they never again allowed themselves to be so unprepared for a long winter. As it is with all people, what the newlyweds had not learned through insight, they were forced to learn through pain. Having learned the hard lesson, my parents gave top priority to buying a big bill of groceries when money was more plentiful at harvest time. This would "tied 'em over," they called it, until they could get a loan each spring for planting a new crop.

A bill of groceries and winter supplies would consist of sugar, salt, pepper, and chili seasoning, a large can of baking powder, boxes of baking soda, a box of corn starch, a fifty-pound bag of flour, a bag of cornmeal, one hundred pounds of potatoes, fifty pounds of dry pinto beans, a large bag of white beans for the sake of variety, boxes of oatmeal, cans of cocoa, several cans of coffee, boxes of tea, a jug of white vinegar, and cases of evaporated milk. They purchased rice in a one-hundred-pound bag from the rice dryer in Weiner.

Matches and kerosene were kept on hand for lighting the lamps and starting a fire in the heating stove. Other necessary items included needles and thread, bullets, hand soap (or lye for making their own soap), boxes of powdered detergent, and a jug of bleach. The same box of detergent used for washing clothes was also used for washing the dishes. Laundry detergent made the dishes so slippery that one could hardly hold on to them.

Items from the pantry were often used for medicine. For a sore throat, gargling with warm salt water was most healing. Salt and baking soda were used for brushing the teeth. Baking soda was also placed on a bee sting, hoping it would neutralize the venom. Fresh meat that needed to be preserved and stored was covered with salt. Vinegar, mixed with water, was also used to combat ear or a yeast infection. Corn starch could sooth a heat rash or a diaper rash when there were no drugstore products available.

Occasionally, a well-established farmer in the community offered to sell his unneeded eggs and milk. Butter could be churned from the heavy cream that rose naturally to the surface of the fresh milk. In case Eva and Levi had a need after their money was spent, they were permitted to keep a running balance at Clark's general store at Uno and pay at a later date. Levi drove past two general stores to shop at Jo Clark's store. I don't know if she was religious at all, but it was a merciful thing that she chose to do for poor families in the community. I'm sure she suffered some losses along the way.

Customers at the general store were enticed to buy a particular small bag of flour that had a desirable washcloth stitched in the seam. The fabric bag itself was laundered and used to dry dishes. The larger bags of flour came in a yard of print fabric that delighted the women who sewed and could not afford to buy fabric. Eva used the beautiful print fabric to make shirts and dresses and saved even the scraps for making quilts. A free wash cloth or dish towel came inside a box of laundry detergent. Boxes of oatmeal often came with a cup or small glass buried inside, and tea came with a much-needed pedestal drinking glass attached to the box.

Eva appreciated the white fabric sacks that held feed for the hogs and sewed them into little girl's panties and slips. It took several bags to make one bedsheet and that resulted in a seam being created in several places on the flat sheet. Our toenails would sometime get snagged in the seams when allowed to grow too long and become jagged.

Wire pliers, a pocket knife, and a pocket watch on a chain were necessities to Levi while a clock, a calendar, an almanac, letter writing supplies, and a bible were among items Eva cherished most. She found it hard to throw away outdated calendars and kept them stored for years. The free Sears and Roebuck catalog offered hours of entertainment as a wish book and provided necessary "wipin' paper" in the outdoor toilet.

Watching Out for One Another

My grandmother Della West was not a wealthy lady but rented out her farmland at Grubbs to a sharecropper for income while she lived as simply as possible. When Grandpa West passed away (shortly after I was born), she graciously allowed my parents to continue farming the land they called Papa's place. In addition, Grandma paid for materials so my father could build a three-bedroom house on the farm.

Daddy and Mike were helped with the building project by one of my mother's retarded brothers, John Horace West. There was no electricity for power tools, so the house was built entirely with hand tools, such as a handsaw and a brace and bit. Hundreds of bolts were used to connect the boards for making rafters. The house was built with no insulation or plumbing, no electricity, and no furnace or ductwork for a heating or cooling system. The unfinished floors had no subflooring, tile, or linoleum. Rolls of gray exterior wrap were unrolled and nailed onto the outside walls in place of siding. My father did a good job building the house considering that he had no carpenter training. Our comfortable house looked presentable inside with drywall and trim work and a good paint job. Each room was painted either light green or dusty rose pink. Right away, my creative little brother added his decorative touch to the walls with a crayon.

Walking with God in the Backwoods

Free-standing wood-burning stoves provided heat in the living room and kitchen. To lessen the danger of a house fire, the dampers on the wood-burning stoves were shut down low for the night, and it soon became very cold. To keep the little ones from freezing, Mama slept in a full-size bed with the little girls while Daddy slept in a full-size bed with the little boys. In that way, they could keep the children covered during the night. It got extremely cold in the bedrooms before morning, and occasionally, my parents found a thin layer of ice in the gallon bucket of drinking water in the kitchen.

Faces and hands were washed in the porcelain wash pan in the kitchen where the water was changed frequently. Bathing could only be done when a bedroom was sufficiently warm to allow for disrobing and washing from a wash pan of water. We were limited to sponge bathing for three months out of each year. In the spring, the galvanized steel bathtub was carried into the house and heated water poured into it. Each person in the family took turns using the same water.

With the heat of summer, flies and mosquitoes filled the house in spite of the fact that we had a screen door and screen wire nailed over the outside of the windows. An ordinary flyswatter was inadequate for the enormous amount of flies that got inside our house. When the flies were especially bad at Grandma West's house, she would turn the dinner plates upside down on the dining table to keep them clean until everyone was seated for a meal. That ritual rarely happened at our house because my parents made generous use of "fly dope."

In the late afternoon, Mama draped a sheet over the kitchen table to cover the items that were kept there. The windows and doors were closed to make the rooms as airtight as possible while a handheld pump dispenser filled with liquid Black Flag was sprayed into each room. As the thick mist settled, house flies and mosquitoes dropped dead on the moist wooden floor.

On especially hot summer nights, it was miserable to lie in the bed, for the mattress held our body heat. A quilt placed on the wooden floor near an open window created an instant bed called a pallet. Lying on a pallet and fanning ourselves with a piece of cardboard was the only relief we got from the heat. We'd be asleep before the late-night air cooled the outdoors and a cool breeze filtered through the rusted screens. Mama got up in the night to put covers over us so we wouldn't wake up shivering from the cold. We were blessed to have a roomy, comfortable house and the beauty of a place to call home.

Knowing our grandmother owned the house and land where we grew up gave my siblings and me a sense of security and was the next best thing to owning our own home. Grandma West sacrificed an income from Papa's place after his death so my family could live rent-free and have a better quality of life. Though this gracious lady was not affectionate, we were blessed daily by the decisions she made, which showed mercy and granted us such loving favor.

> He will fulfill the desire of them that fear him; he also will hear their cry, and will save them.

> —Psalms 145:19

6

I'll Be List'ning
1955

I WAS THE THIRD CHILD of seven, but the only child delivered at home by my dad. He never once referred to that experience in my presence nor at any other time that was known to me. My parents, Levi and Eva, were taught that the discussion of such things was improper. They did not discuss anything of a sensitive nature with their children or in the presence of their children. My mother was sometimes like the English nobility, and if she disapproved of a behavior, she could usually put a stop to it quickly with the curt retort, "That's not proper."

I didn't ask my parents questions about the facts of life or even the circumstances surrounding my birth at home, not even when I became an adult. I did ask Mike many years later,

Mabel Margaret Motes Bufford

and he told me all that he could remember. I was curious during childhood, but I didn't want to be embarrassed, and I didn't want to embarrass my parents; it was just too uncomfortable to talk to my mother or to my dad about personal things. That seems strange, even to me, now that I am in a world where people are guests on talk shows and shocking the world with details of their intimate moments.

When a woman became pregnant, the older people would pass the word discreetly to others by saying that she was "in the family way." If a proper older lady was visiting at the home of a country family and she needed to find the outdoor toilet, she might say to others that she was "going to look at the flowers." In the country, the outhouse was often hidden from view by planting tall flowers nearby. A favorite flower for hiding an outhouse was the hollyhock.

I was given the name Mabel Margaret. Mabel was the name of my mother's favorite sister, and Margaret was the name of President Truman's talented daughter who was a famous singer. Names that began with an *m* had been popular for decades. Many parents had continued to name their baby girls Mary, Margaret, Martha, Mildred, Mae, or Mabel through the 1940s. I did not like my first name, which seemed to be for an *old* person, but I agreed to be called Mabel at the request of Miss Myrth, my first-grade schoolteacher. It lessened the confusion caused by having another Margaret in the classroom.

Miss Myrth and the Pencil Sharpener

In the fall of 1955, Mike went away to college at Arkansas State University in Jonesboro, and I began elementary school in Weiner. As an enthusiastic student, I enjoyed the cheerful classroom with large windows. I was especially fascinated by the pencil sharpener that was affixed to the wall at my level. One day as I stood sharpening my pencil, my teacher, Miss Myrth, came behind me without a word and swatted me on the buttocks with her hand. I didn't know what I had done to deserve a spanking. I immediately turned to walk toward the low table with the tiny chair that I was assigned to occupy. Since she spanked me most of the way to my seat, I supposed that she wanted me to stay seated. Apparently, Miss Myrth did not know that she was supposed to inform me of her intentions, and she certainly did not count aloud to three, like modern people do. Not only had Miss Myrth not given me ample warnings, I was not aware of any instructions being given that would limit my use of the pencil sharpener. Maybe she did give instructions, but I wasn't listening when she informed the class. Whatever the case, I decided to stay seated, keep quiet, and pay attention.

When I told my father about the bewildering incident a few years later, I was surprised to find that he had complained to Miss Myrth. Daddy defended himself, saying, "W'al, I told Miss Myrth that I couldn't keep you in pencils."

Mabel Margaret Motes Bufford

I vaguely remember my father having fussed at home about the high cost of pencils, but that made no more impact on me than if he had fussed about the high cost of groceries. As a child of six, I did not have the capacity to reason that I should limit pencils any more than I could cut back on my eating.

—⟋⟍—

The Washpot and the Rubboard

Wash day was quite an ordeal for my poor mother. Audrey stayed home from school one day each week to help on laundry day by watching her baby brother and sister, Andrew and Kathy. A rip-roaring fire had to be built to heat water to wash clothes. Rather than to heat up the house in hot weather, Mama carried buckets of water from the hand pump to fill a big cast-iron pot in the backyard. She put a load of clothes inside the pot of water and used stove wood to build a fire underneath it. During the time the dirty clothes were presoaking, Mama filled two galvanized-steel washtubs with water. The tubs were set in the early-morning shade directly behind the house.

A portion of an old broomstick had been placed in the simmering pot to poke at the clothes and to lift them out of the washpot when the presoaking was done. Mama used her aluminum dishpan when transferring the hot clothes from the steaming pot to the cold wash water. Within minutes

Walking with God in the Backwoods

of being in the fresh water, the clothes were an acceptable temperature and could be scrubbed on the rubboard. The wash water became warmer as each item was wrung out by hand and then placed in the next tub for rinsing. Two or three marble-sized balls of bluing were dissolved in the rinse water to whiten and brighten the clothes.

The same water was used for each load of clothes, and it worked out fine since the least dirty clothes were washed first. The boys' jeans and my dad's overalls were washed last. Dishpans of clean clothes were carried to the clothesline where they were hung to dry. When the weather was cold, water was heated in the kitchen and carried to tubs on the screened-in back porch. Clothes were hanging on the line each week until the weather became freezing cold. I can remember my mother bringing a pair of overalls into the house that was frozen so stiff that they could stand alone.

After cooking dinner in the wood-burning cook stove, the pressing irons were placed on top of the stove to be heated. There was no permanent press fabric at that time and most items of clothing had to be ironed except Daddy's bib overalls with patches. A nice white shirt that had been starched and pressed and the newest pair of overalls were considered suitable church clothes for poor farmers who went to a country church. On the rare occasion that Daddy bought a pair of trousers, he got size 30 × 30. I remembered his pants size by using word association, for he also had a rifle that was a .30-30.

Playtime at the Bus Stop

The school bus stop was a quarter of a mile, "as the crow flies," through the woods from our house, and our parents finally risked allowing us to wait there without supervision. While my siblings and I waited for the bus, we romped and played beside the county road. There was very little traffic and very little danger. We waved to the road-grader driver as he drove by, leaving a ridge of gravel heaped along the edge of the road. It was as tempting as a sandbox, and we began to play in it. I scooped gravel onto the skirt part of my dress and carried it to the deep ruts left where my dad had pulled off the main road onto our property. "I'm gunna gravel ar driveway," I said with great enthusiasm and purpose. Until the bus arrived, I scurried around dropping to my knees and scooping gravel with both hands onto my skirt and depositing the heavy load into the ruts. I was not aware that the whole front of my dress was dirty. Mama was horrified when she found that I had gone to school in that condition.

Teased at School

"Mabel, Black Label," some of the boys at school would say to me in good-natured teasing. I did not respond to them, but the attention embarrassed me. At that time, our family had no access to a television, so I was unaware of the meaning of that phrase; I feared that it was something bad. Though the teasing was not cruel and there was no lasting harm done, I had discovered that individual attention at school was most often negative. Many years passed before I would discover that my name was associated with that of a waitress named Mabel depicted on a television commercial which advertised beer. In the commercial, a man would call to the waitress from his table, saying, "Mabel, Black Label."

The teasing at school contributed to me rejecting my first name, which then produced a bit of an identity crisis. Throughout my school years, I had two identities. At home and at church, I was called Margaret, and that was who I was most comfortable being.

> Listen, O isles, unto me; and hearken ye people, from
> far; The Lord hath called me from the womb; from the
> bowels of my mother hath he made mention of my name.

—Isaiah 49:1

The Old-Time Religion
1956

WOMEN AND MINORITIES FOUND THE Holy Spirit to be *no respecter of persons*; equality was found in the presence of God. Gifts of the Spirit that were taught in the New Testament era flourished as the Spirit of the Almighty God anointed ministers to preach with passion and power. The new wave of spiritual revival called Pentecost was like the early church in the book of Acts. The Pentecostal believers worshiped God in an exuberant manner, which made them seem odd to Christians in traditional churches. *Holy Rollers* was a derogatory term attributed to the believers who had embraced the fresh outpouring of the Holy Ghost.

The *Assemblies of God* denomination was officially organized in 1914, at a meeting of Pentecostal believers in Hot Springs, Arkansas. The new denomination welcomed anointed women to establish and to pastor churches. Many women were successful in spreading the Gospel while enduring extreme poverty, profound hardships, and gender prejudice.

Many small congregations of Pentecostal people took root in the rural areas of Arkansas. The churches were often small, simple buildings with two outhouses at opposite corners on the back lawn. Often, those churches were along winding gravel roads and nestled among the trees in heavily wooded areas. There were few Pentecostal churches uptown in those days, but God had chosen the poor for they were rich in faith. Pentecost was considered the poor man's religion.

A television set was quite the popular item in the home of prosperous people in the early 1950s. Holiness people preached against the carnal Christians who dared to own one. Overzealous Pentecostal believers chided the guilty ones about the antennae on their roof and referred to it as "devil's horns."

There was a great attempt by the Pentecostal preachers to promote personal purity, which became known as the Holiness Movement. Some people tried so hard to be holy that they became legalistic, which discouraged new converts. My Aunt Ellie dipped snuff, but she carried such a heavy anointing that she could not testify in church without preaching under the anointing of the Holy Spirit. She also carried a white handkerchief to dab at her mouth every few seconds as she

Walking with God in the Backwoods

spoke. The Christian who dipped snuff and chewed tobacco was asked, "Where are you going to spit when you get to heaven?" People stopped asking that question when someone replied, "In your coffee cup."

—ɯ—

Relationships

Mike always knew when our parents had been in a disagreement ending in hurt feelings. Long after Daddy had retired for the night, Mama would sit up late and read her Bible by the light of the kerosene lamp. During dark nights of the soul, reading the Psalms helped her to express her frustration when life became nearly unbearable. The Psalms were a guide to help her pray effectively, to praise the Lord in times of trouble, and to feel hope and faith for a brighter future.

When my parents were newlywed, a kind neighbor gave them an old battery-powered radio, but Levi told Eva to give it away because she and Mike sat while listening to the dramatized stories on it. Levi had protested the unacceptable pastime, calling it "watching the radio." I am sure my mother often felt trapped in the backwoods, for she was truly tied down and cut off from the world.

In Psalms 143, Mama found a remedy for the anguish of her soul. In verses 5 and 6, the psalmist tells what action he took to rescue himself: "I remember the days of old; I meditate on all thy works." While meditating on the goodness of God,

David reviewed the victories of the past and gave attention to the good in the present. "I muse on the works of thy hands," he said as he took note of the beauty of nature and all God had created. "I stretch forth my hands unto thee," he said. Like David the Psalmist, Mama reached out to the one consistent source and found that God was faithful to her personally and available at all times.

The Lady Preacher

Driving from Newport in an old pickup truck, Sister Velma Turnage held meetings in an abandoned one-room church in the community called Haw Thicket, a few miles from Waldenburg. At one time, the building, which was situated in a dense grove of trees, had been the Harmony Grove Schoolhouse. They chose to keep the name Harmony Grove, for it was the perfect name for the little Pentecostal church that occupied such a serene area beneath a canopy of green leaves.

Sister Velma was powerfully anointed by the Holy Ghost and seemed somewhat masculine to me because she talked so loud when she preached. She was the opposite of my timid mother and any other woman I knew, for she was comfortable with being the focus of attention. Her husband came with her occasionally, but he was so quiet and unassuming that I hardly remember him.

Sister Velma was a matronly woman who wore her long brown hair twisted into an enormous bun on the back of her head, which was held in place with hair pins. The same distinctive style was worn by so many other Pentecostal women that it came to be known as a Pentecostal bun. It was not unusual to see a woman in church so overcome by the power of the Holy Ghost that she shouted while her bun came falling down and hairpins went flying in every direction.

In the 1950s, most houses and church buildings had electricity. Some of the country churches had acquired a fan or two—but not this one. It was very hot inside. Being accustomed to the heat, all church women dressed modestly. A simple cotton dress that Mama called the shirt-waist dress was a common style that Sister Velma and most Pentecostal women wore. It was gathered at the waist and had sleeves that folded above the elbow like a cuff. Many of the country women had a Singer sewing machine in their home, and they sewed their own dresses.

—✹—

Having Church

The temperature was sweltering, and the humidity was high. The Holy Ghost was moving like a heat wave on this hot summer evening in Arkansas, and those in the congregation had determined not to miss it. Babies were passed from person to person and enjoyed affection from many people, especially from the teenage girls who went to great lengths to entertain them. This was a special treat for the little ones who were not given enough attention at home. I can remember being a little child and a teenager keeping me quiet and entertained during church by allowing me to rummage through her purse. Her purse was as exciting as a treasure chest to me.

We enjoyed lively Pentecostal song services with Sister Velma walking back and forth as she beat on a tambourine in a forceful, rhythmic manner with the heel of one hand. Accompanied by an acoustic guitar, she sang at the top of her lungs. I too sang loudly with the congregation and made up words that sounded similar to what others were singing. Even then—before I was old enough to follow in the hymn book—I enjoyed feeling the presence of God.

When Sister Velma was behind the pulpit, she was very commanding. She paused occasionally to catch her breath and to retrieve the dangling handkerchief that was tucked in her belt. While Sister Velma wiped away the perspiration that ran down the side of her face, I sat spellbound, eager for her to continue. "We are a peculiar people with an unpopular message," she admonished. "We cannot love the world and the world will not love us."

—◈—

The Elephant

Several times a year, the church would invite an evangelist or guest speaker to hold a series of meetings every night for two weeks. When the Pentecostal meetings were called a revival, everyone knew the services would last until *whenever*. As the

Walking with God in the Backwoods

meetings ran long, the rowdy boys often went outside and romped in the churchyard, played tag, and scuffled in the darkness. The children in my family were not allowed that freedom. One boy said his mother always sat near the front and never looked back.

Teenage boys and young men hung around the open doorway of the dimly lit church. In the edge of the darkness, they hovered, peering in to see what was happening. Watching the Holy Rollers was cheap entertainment for the poor boys that had neither girlfriends nor money to attend the movie theater in the small town of Weiner.

During a lull in the service one Sunday night, I became aware that I was very thirsty. My attention span was not very long, and I reasoned that being thirsty was an acceptable excuse to move about during the service. I stepped outside the door into the darkness with the intention of walking to the iron handled pump in the church yard and pumping a cool drink of water for myself. It was later in the evening and much darker than I expected. The billowing cigarette smoke coming from the direction of young men congregated nearby added eeriness. My heart was pounding as I stood still on the porch of the church and waited for my eyes to adjust to the darkness. I hoped that bravery would descend upon me, but it did not; I was too afraid to go farther. A slender boy in obvious distress rushed to his friends who were standing nearest to me. He appeared to be about twelve years old.

"Sump'en...tried to get me...out thar...in the dark," he struggled to say between gasps.

"What was it?" his friend asked with a tone of concern.

"I dun' know...but hit wuz big...like uh...elephant!"

Uh...elephant? I said to myself. Suddenly, I was no longer thirsty. I was eager to get back inside the church to sit in safety.

—∿—

Transportation Problems

During the following week, our old car which had been dependable suddenly would not run anymore. Upon investigation, my dad determined the cause of the problem.

"Somebody put sugar in the gas tank." Daddy sighed wearily. "It probably happened at the church."

We had no phone to call a law officer to report the incident and no other automobile to drive. Having no contact with the church people, we did not know if other automobiles had been vandalized as well.

During the time we were without transportation, my dad went by tractor and wagon to shop for groceries at Clark's store at Uno. When he needed to conduct business or run an errand in the town of Weiner or Grubbs, the wagon could be disconnected and left at home. For weeks at a time, Mama stayed home with the little ones without getting to talk to other people.

Walking with God in the Backwoods

Mama appreciated the mail carrier and the postal service all the more because she could place an envelope of coins in the rural mailbox a half mile away from the house to buy stamps. She was a faithful letter writer and appreciated the personal letters which were like a lifeline coming through the post office from the outside world.

There had been another time when we did not have a functioning automobile. I can remember being about four years old when my dad bought a farm tractor for the first time. He hooked it to the wagon, and we went visiting beyond Grubbs to Grandma West's house. It must have been about ten miles or more from our house near Flag Slough. Fortunately, I was too young to remember much about our life before we got the John Deere tractor, and the mode of transportation for my family was a team of farm mules to pull the wagon.

One of my older cousins, Mary Ann, the daughter of Uncle John Henry wrote to me about her memories in Arkansas before they moved to Chicago. She said, "Your mom and dad and you kids were so much fun to visit…I remember coming home from church in a horse-drawn wagon with Uncle Levi at the reins. I was very small. The Lord was drawing me to himself through those experiences. I am so happy about the great heritage of Christ your parents gave us."

The Baptist church had a new building two miles from our house at the intersection of two gravel roads. The small church, simply called Cooper and Hanes, was built with

109

concrete blocks that were about eight-by-twelve inches in size and three inches thick. It had a poured concrete floor that seemed very nice and modern to us at the time and was so sturdy that it could be used as a storm shelter. We went by tractor and wagon at least once that summer to attend a church service there. Having realized that our family was among the poorest of the poor, it was no small embarrassment for me as an eight-year-old to arrive in such a humble manner. Since other people had nice automobiles, the wagon was a symbol of poverty to me.

Writing about the incident has caused me to wonder about the young men who planned and executed such a devilish prank of pouring sugar into a poor family's gas tank while they worshipped the Lord. After they matured, they probably asked God to forgive their youthful transgressions. Without transportation for about a year, my whole family was thrust into instant hardship. Like a pebble tossed into a pond of still water, my lifelong memories of being without transportation are like the rippling effect, still in motion, from that one solitary act.

> Yea, and all that will live godly in
> Christ Jesus shall suffer persecution.
>
> —2 Timothy 3:12

Gathering Home
1957

WHILE THE 1950S HAD BEEN a time of renewal and prosperity for the majority of American cities, especially the industrialized cities in the northern states, our secluded farm in the backwoods of Arkansas was like a place frozen in time.

A mass exodus of young farm laborers was assimilated into the northern factories that required no experience and little education. Broken marriages often resulted when a Christian heritage was abandoned, in addition to the farm lifestyle, by the many Southerners who were in an ardent quest for better wages.

Poverty, which sentenced men to hard physical labor, seemed to be especially cruel to women and children. By virtue of their more sensitive and delicate qualities, they were denied the dignity that nature had requisitioned for them. Only the very young children, happily engrossed in play, were oblivious to the intense shame of their poverty.

As I was growing up, my family enjoyed a few visits from relatives who were employed in the automobile industry in Michigan. The factory workers were former residents of Arkansas who had packed their family and their belongings in an old pickup truck and headed north. The loved ones left behind were torn between a desire for a better life and a fear of the evils that could possibly befall those who dared to step into unfamiliar territory and risk the unknown.

Among our visitors, we found an occasional disillusioned soul who longed for open spaces, baying hound dogs, and the solitude of tilling the soil. However, the factory worker could not reconcile his personal desire with the image of barefoot children in tattered clothes spending their summer days playing in the powdery dirt at the end of long cotton rows.

The Michigan factory workers who visited our farm were enjoying a vacation. The luxury of travel was not affordable or convenient for farm families nor was it ever considered a possibility. It was noticed that our visitors were driving nice cars. Any car that could be trusted to make a trip of one thousand miles was worthy of envy. Poor farm families usually acquired an old automobile that could be used for a few years before it had to be exiled to a designated area behind the house to be held prisoner by the underbrush and briars. My parents did a better job than most impoverished people of disposing of their old automobiles because they enjoyed having pretty flowers in the yard.

My family sat in rapt attention, patiently enduring subtle attempts by our guests to coax us into their new lifestyle. It was a grand diversion to let the imagination soar as the stories of great possibilities unfurled. Though the conversation was peppered with hints of crime rates and crowded housing projects, the faraway factories represented a promise of affluence. Like the story of Moses leading God's people to the land of Canaan, Michigan was considered the promised land—having a promise of prosperity. Unlike Canaan, Michigan didn't always feel like home. The relatives were often torn between two states. During a layoff from the factory, they might even move back for awhile, for Arkansas was *home*.

—∞—

Cowboys and Indians

We were surprised one summer day when my dad came home with two sets of *cowboy holster with guns*. He gave one to Joe and one to Andrew. Daddy had also purchased the necessary supply of ammunition for the cap pistols. The gifts were not for a special occasion—just a time that my dad had a little extra money—and that was a rare occurrence. All the little girls in the family enjoyed the pistols as well.

We had a wonderful time playing *cowboys and Indians* when our relatives returned to Weiner and came to visit. Uncle Tom and Aunt Elizabeth had a big family of seven children with one set of twins. The twins, Jane and Janice, were about my age. The cousins organized our game of cowboys and Indians, giving each of us the name of a character from the Wild West. One boy would be Davy Crockett, one would be Daniel Boone, and there was Gene Autry, Roy Rogers, and Dale Evans. We ran out of characters, and I was the only cowgirl without a name. I was not familiar with the characters my cousins saw on television and was therefore of no assistance in thinking of a character name.

"I know," exclaimed Janice, "you can be Betty Crocker! That sounded like a nice Western name to me.

The Flying Jenny

A *flying jenny* was the first toy I can remember my dad made for us. It was made by fastening a long two-by-eight board on top of a stump with a large bolt. It could be pushed around in a circle like a merry-go-round. One child could sit on each end of the board and ride while a third child would run in a circle pushing it. All children not participating were kept out of the way because the twirling board could hit them in the head and knock them out cold. Little hands could be pinched between the board and the stump, making it a very dangerous toy that required parental supervision. Needless to say, my mother made sure it was soon disassembled.

Playing with Feathers

Our house sat less than two feet off the ground and was open all the way around, making it light underneath and allowing the small animals to wander in and out. Our dogs and cats often lay under the house to give birth to their little ones. We crawled underneath the house to check on the puppies and kittens and discovered that being there was somewhat like being in a different world. Hills and valleys were created under the house where the free-range chickens had scratched deep holes for lounging in the cool, soft dirt.

For lack of toys, we often used our imagination to transform whatever was available into suitable entertainment for ourselves. Feathers found lying on the ground left by the many chickens that were wandering about were transformed into imaginary people. A magnificent landscape where our feather families could form a village was provided under the house. The long feathers became a mom or dad while the smaller feathers became their children. A canning jar lid made a fine little car for our imaginary people. When we filled the lid with dirt and packed it down with our palm, the feathers could stand upright in it. My younger brother, Joe, brought a bucket of water under the house and filled a

Mabel Margaret Motes Bufford

hole for the creation of a pond. In that way, the imaginary family could drive in their cars to the pond to be baptized. Joe enjoyed having the honors of baptizing the feather people for he could recite all the right words before dunking them under. We spent most of the hot month of August under the house where it was cooler, crawling around, building roads for what had become a large population of feather people.

While we were occupied under the house all afternoon, Mama enjoyed sewing on the pedal sewing machine as she watched baby Kathy who played on the floor at her feet. Mama could easily hear us talking through the gaping knot holes in the floor just above our head. We were content, and she was blessed with guilt-free personal time. As baby Kathy napped on the bed, Mama wrote letters and read in the Bible. At the end of the day, we would come crawling out from underneath the house with our clothing full of powdery dirt.

We contracted the whooping cough that summer. Little Mildred had a bad coughing spell one day while "playin' feathers," and Mama had to crawl under the house and drag her out.

Each morning during the hottest part of summer, Mama pumped enough water to fill a large galvanized-steel bathtub, which set in the hot sun in the backyard. By the end of the day, the water was warm enough for bathing. One by one, each of her dirty little children could take a turn in the bathtub. Only the baby was stripped naked out of doors where others might see her. My sisters Audrey, Mildred, and I could sit on the edge and wash our feet and legs or get in with our clothes on. Except for the pesky mosquitoes, it was pleasant to be in an outdoor hot tub.

Trouble in Paradise

Joe, just a year and a half younger, followed close behind me as we both crawled on our belly underneath the house to continue our fantasy game with feathers. As soon as I got fully beyond the immediate area of entry, I looked toward the hilly landscape of the imaginary village. I was surprised and dismayed to find we had an intruder just five feet away. I stopped immediately and warned, "Thar's a snake, Joe, get out!" By that time, Joe was beside me and he too had spotted it. The black snake was lying very still, so Joe and I calmly inched our way backward while watching the snake closely. If it had slithered toward us, we would have knocked ourselves unconscious in our hurry to get out from underneath the house.

"Let's get a hoe and kill 'em," I said to Joe. Being in agreement, we both ran to grab our cotton-chopping hoe, which was stored underneath the front porch. We crawled back under the house with long-handled hoes extended before us. From a prone position, we tried to chop the snake but could not lift the garden hoe high enough to strike hard. It squirmed away each time one of us tried to hold it down with a hoe. The snake finally slithered away in haste. After Joe and I came out from underneath the house, we realized that we had placed ourselves in a dangerous position. If it had been a poisonous snake, it might have fought back by striking at us; if it had attempted to strike us, we could not have gotten out of his range in time. We were fortunate that the snake was not vicious and made no attempt to defend itself by attacking us.

I never went back underneath the house to play. The memory of the snake marred the beauty of our fantasyland and caused the magic of make-believe to vanish. Joe and I informed the other children about the snake, but Mildred and Andrew kept playing under the house. They determined to be more careful and watched constantly for the dreaded snakes, which move silently.

On days that we didn't play in the dirt, my sisters and I still got dusty up to our knees from walking barefoot while wearing dresses. On those days, Audrey, Mildred, and I could wash our feet in the tub outdoors by wading around in the water while fully clothed. As we got older, we bathed indoors only.

—∿∿—

Hazards of Play

During a game of *kick-the-can*, my barefoot was cut by the sharp edge on a rusted tin can. Mama poured kerosene over the gaping wound, and the bleeding stopped shortly. She had a home remedy for almost every ailment. Mama warned us of

Walking with God in the Backwoods

the danger of getting lockjaw from such an injury. Though she was greatly concerned, there was to be no trip to the doctor for a tetanus shot. (We didn't play that game again.)

While running barefoot in the yard on a hot summer day, Audrey calmly told me that she had been bitten by a black snake and showed me the teeth marks one top of her foot. It was not swelling, but I suggested that we should go in the house and tell Mama right away. Mama became alarmed and went into a frenzy of activity. I had never seen my mother hurry before. A poisonous snake bite was one of the things she feared most, yet she had no tobacco to put on it for medicine. Being a good Christian, Daddy had given up chewing tobacco long ago.

Mama led Audrey quickly to the tub in the yard and began stripping her clothes off and "washed her up" as fast as she could. Audrey was a very modest child, as all of us were, and it was very embarrassing for her. Mama grabbed a towel from the clothesline and threw it around Audrey and rushed her into the house to get dressed as quickly as possible.

Mama had no phone to call for help and no way to transport Audrey to a hospital. She grabbed baby Kathy, praying aloud as she went, and herded all of us down the long driveway toward the main road. She knew she could get help from the nearest neighbor or someone who might be driving by. Halfway to the gravel road, Mama took time to look at Audrey's foot again. It still was not swollen and had not changed in appearance. With relief, we turned back toward the house. I was not aware of Mama ever being "in a hurry" again all the years of her life.

Gift Giving

While my father was out on errands, he'd watch for pretty flowers like daffodils in the springtime that were left where an old house had burned or had been abandoned. He'd go back later with a shovel and dig some of the flowers up and bring them to my mother. They both shared a love for beautiful flowers and tended them carefully.

My father was not one to buy gifts for Christmas. My mother would usually prompt him to get the children something. My parents had grown up at a time when a Christmas gift was a small brown paper bag containing an orange, an apple, and a handful of nuts and a few pieces of hard candy. An orange was a rare treat because oranges were not grown in Arkansas.

One Christmas, my little sisters, Mildred and Kathy, got a small doll. My younger brothers, Joe and Andrew, got flashlights while my older sister, Audrey, and I got a comb and hairbrush set. My oldest brother, Mike, had gone to Memphis and was working his way through college. I doubt that he got anything for Christmas from us, for he was such a practical and thrifty person that he would have fussed at us for wasting our money. I don't think my parents ever bought Christmas

Walking with God in the Backwoods

gifts for each other. A comb and brush was a necessity, and a flashlight certainly was not a waste of money. Everyone liked to have a flashlight under the pillow as they slept—in case of distress in the night. It was extremely dark in the country where there was no electricity for farm lights. The flashlight was a handy thing to have when getting up in the darkness to light the kerosene lamp.

> Then they cried unto the Lord in their trouble, and he delivered them out of their distresses.

—Psalms 107:6

9

When the Saints Go Marching In 1958

BY THE TIME WE HAD transportation again, the Pentecostals had a different location, but they had kept the same name. A local farmer had donated property alongside another county road in the community for the new church to be built. It was also a wooded area that was almost as scenic as the location they had before. All who attended the new church referred to it affectionately as "Harmony Grove," and not by its denominational affiliation. It wasn't a fancy church, but it did have four Sunday school rooms; there was one on each side of the foyer and one on each side of the podium. The floors were bare wood with no vinyl covering or carpet. If children were permitted to move about during the service, the sound of their footsteps could easily distract and disturb others.

My dad, Audrey, and I arrived early for our first time to attend a church service in the new building in 1958. It was also the first time for the new pastor, Brother James Bittle, and he too arrived early. He was a single young man from Newport and very pleasant in manner and appearance. Brother James invited his good friend who was graduating from high school to come to the church and lead songs and provide music on his acoustic guitar, for we had no other person who could do it. Everyone enjoyed Brother James and his teenaged friend, Noel Madison. They were good role models for my younger brothers and the other little boys in the church.

The church did not have pews, but someone had arranged to salvage padded theater seats that were being discarded from the movie theater in Weiner. They were very comfortable, and it was convenient to lift the seats up during times that we were standing to allow for more space. The somewhat ragged seats were connected one to another but were not fastened to the floor. Occasionally, a rambunctious child would climb over the back of a seat and knock a whole row of empty seats over. As soon as the church could afford a truck load of smooth lumber, Daddy and the other men of the church built sturdy pews.

The Church Ladies

In addition to their bibles, women arrived at the church carrying handheld fans during the summer months. The fans were made of a thin piece of cardboard, about six-by-seven inches in size, affixed to a flat wooden stick. The fans were simple in design, but they had scenic pictures on the front that were as beautiful as a postcard. The women didn't mind that an ad for a funeral home was printed on the back of each fan. Like souvenirs of memorable events, the fans had been collected from the funerals of loved ones. Being useful and appreciated, the fans were used year after year. You would certainly pity the poor child who ruined his mama's fan.

Mothers, young and old, sat patiently in the congregation, continuously fanning the babies and small children who wallowed on their lap. Mothers taught their children to be quiet out of necessity, for there was no nursery for the little ones in the country churches. Young mothers rarely took their babies outside the church building for lack of being able to control them. If an older child was taken out of the church, you could be sure that they were spanked soundly. Mothers of that generation were of the persuasion that if a child needs a whoopin', you give it to him hard enough that you won't have to do it again for a long time.

If a small child was carried out of the church, all the other children smiled at each other in amusement as they listened expectantly for the wailing cry in the distance.

Like a rite of initiation, being spanked was a natural and acceptable occurrence.

"Dancing in the Spirit" is what we called it when my mother got caught up in the spirit and quietly danced before the Lord like David the Psalmist had done in the Old Testament. Going to church was entertaining when the spirit moved on others, and it was meaningful to see people deeply touched when something ministered to their spirit.

—m—

The Order of the Service

Pentecostal churches were often the lowest in attendance in the community, but there were many of them. People who were prosperous and desired influence in the community chose to attend the more formal churches that offered prestige. I grew up in the Harmony Grove church which had a congregation of thirty to fifty people. Though each person was valued, anyone who could sing or play an instrument was a great asset to the church.

At each church service, anyone in the congregation who wanted to join together was invited to sing in the choir. Several people would rise and walk onto the one-step platform to make up an impromptu choir. The choice of songs was decided as they went along by the choir members who made suggestions. There were no practice sessions and no tryouts. They knew that any talent would minister to the

Walking with God in the Backwoods

congregation when it was anointed by the Holy Ghost, and without the Holy Ghost's anointing, their efforts would not minister at all.

There were few people who had a talent for singing. Those having talent were soon recognized and persuaded to "sing specials" and to lead the choir. Pentecostal children enjoyed the catchy tunes with a fast beat and got involved in worshipping God with continuous handclapping through each song. As the song service came to an end, the boys and girls turned their red palms upright to assess the damage. They compared their tingling hands among themselves and sat down with a satisfied smile. It was a small price to pay for "havin' church."

Several testimonies of God's goodness were a regular part of every service. Each time, a different individual was asked to lead in testimonies. The person chosen at random stood behind the pulpit and gave his own testimony first and then encouraged others to give theirs. Having church was not like a spectator sport—everyone could participate. Even the children were allowed to practice the spiritual discipline of confessing the Lord Jesus as their Savior and proclaiming His goodness in a public setting. The church provided a safe place for the young and for the babes in Christ to gain boldness. Hearing the testimonies of God's provision and His faithfulness produced enduring faith in the heart of all who were in attendance.

The prayer requests of the congregation were taken by yet another person. He too stood behind the pulpit giving his own prayer request and then he would ask if there were other needs; after the spoken requests were made known, that individual would ask if there were any unspoken requests. Not everyone wanted their business known and would signify with an upraised hand that they had an unspoken request. As soon as the leader began to pray, the room was buzzing with the sound of corporate prayers, petitions, and praises to the Lord. Silence came back to the room gradually after a few minutes.

Prayer was serious business among the poor people who had no health insurance and no money to pay for hospital bills, doctor bills, or medicine. Some people prayed silent prayers while many people prayed loud, powerful prayers. Each person called upon the Lord in the way that was most compatible with their personality.

The Altar Call

At the end of the sermon, an invitation was given for those who would like to be converted to the Lord Jesus Christ to come forward. Such an invitation was known as the "altar call." When the Holy Ghost was drawing a person to Christ, that person was likely to feel a sensation of heaviness inside their spirit called conviction. To suddenly become conscious of the weight of one's own sinfulness can be described as a feeling of desperation. The uppermost thought in the mind of the convicted individual is to get to the altar for relief or to escape from the presence of the Holy Ghost by leaving the church. When the person who felt Holy Ghost conviction was genuinely sorrowful for his sins, he often collapsed on the altar in tearful repentance. Those who responded to the altar call "got saved."

The homemade altar was longer and lower than a bench. The old-timers referred to the altar as the "mourner's bench." A glossy finish on the stained wood detained droplets of tears and caused them to glisten in the glare from the naked lightbulbs overhead. Those who prayed through to spiritual victory often left a puddle of tears on the altar.

There is a big difference between attending church and "havin' church"—one is a ritual and one is a relationship; one is a habit and the other is a happening. Having church is an experience that initiates a change in one's life.

A Stumbling Block

Some young men who wished to receive the gift of salvation were hindered from going forward by their buddies who fidgeted nervously on the backseat and left the service in feigned amusement. The buddies huddled in the darkness outside the windows, snickering and pitying their poor friends who remained inside and vulnerable. For that reason, there were very few young men who made a decision for Christ and attended church regularly.

When no one responded to the altar call, the pastor said, "Let's jest come up front for a season of prayar." That particular time of prayer could last anywhere from five minutes to two hours; it depended on the moving of the Holy Ghost. *Prayin' through* was the term used to explain the activity that was involved in the long amount of time spent at the altar. During those long sessions of prayer, the saintly elders of the church gathered around the needy individuals and "laid hands on 'em." While praying vibrant prayers like a New Testament disciple, they ordered the evil spirits to flee from people and commanded tumors and illnesses to leave. As a result of their praying with power and taking authority over the enemy, many people were delivered from life-controlling addictions to liquor and tobacco, and many people walked away healed.

Through the Slough

A special effort had to be made to visit our farm, especially during the rainy season. People didn't just drop in at our house because they were passing through the neighborhood. We lived about six miles from the nearest paved road. Our driveway was a dirt road through a slough with standing water which caused us to go a farther distance in an attempt

Walking with God in the Backwoods

to stay on high ground. What should have been a distance of a fourth of a mile became a half of a mile of winding tractor ruts through the muddy woods in the spring time.

Though my father had purchased a used truck, it could not be driven to our house in the winter or the spring. We parked the truck in the edge of the woods at the main road and walked to the house. The one walking at the head of the line assessed the best route while all others marched behind in single file. Rubber boots were a necessity for us. While wading through the water that was about four inches deep, we sank an extra couple inches into the mud with each step. Sometimes, we splashed water higher than our boots and the girls' dress tails were wet and so were a few inches of the boys' pants legs. My sisters and I had areas on the back of our skinny legs that were red and chafed where the wet boots had rubbed against our bare skin as we walked.

One morning when we got on the school bus, Shelia Craft scooted over toward the window so I could sit with her. She looked down toward my knees and said with a compassionate tone, "You're wet." When I looked down, it was as if I was seeing myself for the first time. Though I didn't answer her, I thought, *Yeah, I guess I am.*

After school, we had to navigate our way back through the slough to get home. As we were carefully testing the waters to determine the best course to take, our neighbor, Jake Willbanks, a single young man, suddenly walked up behind us, wearing knee-high rubber boots. He was on the way to

Mabel Margaret Motes Bufford

our house so he could ask our father about something. We had never encountered a man in the woods or in the slough, and we were rarely in the position of conversing with an adult. Our father was most often with us in a public situation, and he did all the talking. With us being naturally shy and in this awkward situation, we hardly knew what to say to Jake. With little more than a greeting, he suggested to Audrey that he could carry her through the water and lifted her up before she had time to answer him. Falling in line behind him, we marched quickly with the water splashing, rather than waiting to see if he intended to carry each individual across the slough. We felt embarrassed with his being there, and he probably felt uncomfortable with us as well. He set Audrey down immediately upon reaching solid ground and walked briskly ahead without a word. The incident left us feeling bewildered and vulnerable as we walked slowly toward the house in silence. We knew he chose to carry Audrey because she was pretty. By the time we arrived at home, the visitor was already gone by way of a different route.

The children in my family were not social people, and we were uncomfortable with those outside our family. We didn't get very many visitors unless it was our relatives or a few children from church. I only remember one lady in our community coming to visit my mother during my childhood. Hedy Bryant brought her two children to visit at least two times when they were elementary school age. My mother had too much work to do and had little time to cultivate

Walking with God in the Backwoods

friendships. She cooked three meals a day and made corn bread or biscuits from scratch for each meal. My parents did not just raise one vegetable garden, but they raised "truck patches" which had to be maintained, harvested, and canned to provide food for the coming winter.

Our neighbor to the north, named Gene Mitchell, made it a point to walk to our house through the backwoods and across a twenty-acre field once each summer. He took great delight in teasing my little brothers by threatening to steal our watermelons. The first time Mr. Mitchell asked what they would do about it, Joe and Andrew answered him quickly, in unison, "We'll shoot you."

Mr. Mitchell laughed heartily when he got a rise out of the shy little boys. His visits did little toward eliminating the Motes children's distrust of outsiders. Joe and Andrew's social skills slowly improved as they learned to tolerate the teasing. When it ceased to be fun for Mr. Mitchell, he abandoned the yearly ritual.

The standing water in the slough disappeared in the heat of summer, and it was a pleasant walk down the winding driveway that made a dark tunnel through the dense woods. Though there was an open field on two sides of our house, woods surrounded the fields, so the farm and the house could not be seen from the main road. My mother liked it that way. She did best with lots of alone time and the predictability of a daily routine. Anything outside her usual routine had to be planned for, and she would get up earlier to prepare for it.

Lazy Summer Days

By the middle of a long summer, our home could have been mistaken for an abandoned house had it not been for the beaten path that encircled it. We didn't own a lawn mower to keep the grass and weeds under control. When the tall grass encouraged the mosquitoes to multiply, Daddy would buy a bag of DDT and cast it about by the handful to lie on top of the grass. We didn't know until years later that DDT was a very dangerous product.

There was a particular kind of grass or weed near the house that looked a lot like clover called sheepshire. Audrey occasionally carried a slice of corn bread out into the yard and sat down to eat it along with the delicate plant, which had a tangy flavor.

Daddy carried home samples of a special grass called Bermuda and planted it in the front yard. This type of grass was ideal for people who had no lawn mower and no expectation of getting one. The special grass was softer, lower growing, and spread quickly. Eventually, it did spread over the whole front yard and gave a nicer appearance. It was certainly better than the tall grass and weeds which we had in the years before.

During Mike's break from college, he enjoyed a lazy summer day lying on the wooly grass with his siblings in the front yard. He directed our attention to a chicken hawk gliding passed in the bright blue sky. Soon, each of his siblings were lying on their back and gazing upward at the billowing clouds that hovered low. With the magic of a child's imagination, the sky could be transformed into a fantasy playground as we delighted in seeing the hint of familiar shapes in the cotton-soft clouds.

Mike was a mature person who was interested in the weather and the condition of the crops. Our cotton fields were as dry as a sun-bleached bone, and the leaves on the cotton stalks hung limp. It seemed that all nature was in agony and crying out for water. Mike gathered all the children around to sit with him on the wooden gate to the cow lot while watching the sky, hoping to see a rain cloud. He was always strong in the matter of prayer, even as a teenager. "Help me pray for rain," Mike encouraged us. We didn't really know how to pray a beautiful prayer, so we didn't say anything. It was nice that he had confidence in us that we could influence God—if we prayed. Mike taught us by his example to have great confidence in our Heavenly Father who cares about everything that concerns us.

—🙣—

The Cat

As usual during the summer, Daddy was plowing with his tractor in the field all day. He drove the tractor home at noon to eat a hot meal and then left again. Mama was always occupied with housework and chores. "None of those things are any fun," we protested. We were bored and wished we could go somewhere.

The old pickup truck was parked in the yard, but Mama couldn't drive. Daddy had named the truck Ole Lightning. It was painted two-tone, with dark blue on the bottom and white on the top portion of the cab. He said it probably looked like a streak of lightning when he drove fast down the gravel road.

We climbed all over the truck and played inside it. It was neat how the gears could be shifted without the key to turn the switch on. One child was chosen to steer while all the others pushed. We got the truck rolling however slowly, as we anticipated our turn to drive. When we heard an animal screech, we realized that we had rolled the tire over one of our cats. The cat must have been lying asleep in the shade underneath the truck when the tire rolled over his tail and back legs. In horror, we rushed to the aid of the cat which was lying very still and helpless on the grass. We were so sorry about what we had done and wanted desperately to help him to recover.

Mildred ran as fast as she could to the cow lot where Mama was milking the cow to tell her of the desperate situation. Rather than dropping everything to come to our assistance as we expected, Mama found Mildred's wide-eyed hysterical expression to be amusing; she just chuckled and continued milking. Mildred ran back to where the pitiful animal was lying on the grass. It was up to us to save the cat's life.

Joe had heard at school of a procedure called artificial resuscitation and ran quickly to get a tire pump. We had seen what a tire pump could do for a limp inner tube. Andrew held the nozzle end of the tire pump in the cat's mouth and the girls prayed while Joe pumped air as hard and fast as he could. After a few minutes, the cat jumped up and ran away from us. We were so relieved for God had answered our prayers and helped us to save the cat's life. The cat might have died the next day, but he certainly didn't die that day.

The Puppy

We were warned each fall to watch for stray dogs and small animals in the woods that might have rabies, but we never saw any. A warning was sent home with school students telling the symptoms of rabid animals. Our dogs had become ill, and all had died except for Mildred's little puppy. He was sick and was kept isolated in the corn crib in the barn where Mildred carried a plate of leftover food regularly to feed him. When she placed the food near his mouth one day, he attempted to bite her. She became alarmed at the wild look in his eyes and noticed there were bubbles around his mouth. Mildred wondered what that could be on his mouth and then remembered having heard the words *foaming at the mouth*.

Feeling suddenly afraid of him, she backed out and slammed the door shut. She ran back to the house to tell Daddy about her puppy's strange behavior.

"My puppy tried to bite me, and he's foamin' at the mouth," she said with alarm. Upon hearing Mildred's urgent report, Daddy calmly got up without saying a word and got his gun. As Daddy headed to the barn, Mildred ran along behind him pleading, "Don't shoot 'em, Daddy."

"Get back to the house," Daddy told her in a serious tone. Mildred stopped and waited sadly for the inevitable sound of gunfire.

—⁓—

Farm Dogs

Mama didn't like smelly dogs lying on the porch or hanging around the screen doors, and it was nice that they were gone. She wouldn't think of letting them inside the house, and the dogs knew instinctively that their place was outdoors. Daddy believed that keeping two or three big dogs was a necessity for they served the purpose of guarding the property. They gave us ample warning of any approaching man or beast; they also gave fright to intruders and dissuaded them from criminal activity. The big dogs were not pets, and we did not often touch them for they were plagued by large blood-sucking ticks that had attached to their skin and extended beyond the fur as they filled with blood. All the Motes children liked puppies, which were like living toys. It was hard for us to believe that a puppy could grow up to become such a nasty ole farm dog.

When Daddy returned from business in town, we would rush to meet him in case he had bought some candy. Even when he didn't bring candy to us, he always brought Mama up-to-date news from the outside world. Like a news anchorman, Daddy would give a detailed report about the places he had been, what he saw, who he talked to, and what they said. Though we had walked away, we overheard him telling Mama of having seen a man in Weiner that had puppies to give away. With great delight, we rushed to Daddy and begged to go immediately to pick out one, or two or perhaps one for each of the six children.

Mama began fussing at the prospect of a pack of dogs to feed. She laid down the law, "Don't get more than two, and don't get any girl dogs." Mama did not explain why not to get girl dogs, for she wasn't really instructing us as much as she was limiting Daddy. She had no idea that the enemy of my soul would use her words to torment me with the thought that girls were somehow less desirable and I was inferior in some way.

Daddy hovered over us as we clamored about the box full of puppies. He told us which ones were boy dogs and which were girl dogs. Since we could only choose two dogs, we allowed Joe and Andrew to pick the puppies they would like to take. Hunting dogs were more for boys anyway, but we gave our opinions about which puppies they should pick. Andrew chose a docile black and white puppy that Daddy said would make a fine hunting dog. "We'll call him Trailer," Daddy said. That sounded fine to us. Joe seemed partial to the more aggressive puppy that growled as it was being lifted out of the box. "We could call him Growler," Daddy suggested. And so it was to be that the temperamental brown-spotted dog was chosen for Joe.

True to form, the foul-tempered Growler eventually bit a neighbor girl named Rita who had walked a half of a mile to visit with Audrey. The dog's bite did not bring blood to the surface of the skin but left a large bruise on the back of her upper leg. None of our dogs had been to a veterinarian for shots. Rita might have been told by her parents that she could not visit at our house again or maybe she made the decision on her own; however, she never came back. In those days, there were no lawyers encouraging people to sue others. If the dog bite had been more serious, then the two fathers would certainly have discussed it. Soon afterward, the decision was made to take Ole Growler into the woods and put him to rest before he could seriously injure a child. Ferocious dogs and the possibility of rabies discouraged children from wandering about in the community.

Keeping a pack of barking watchdogs around the house gave a backwoodsman a sense of power by giving him warning of strangers approaching. He needed a chance to assess the situation and to consider his position. It gave him time to act rather than to simply react. The dogs could stop a friend or foe at the edge of the property and give time for the homeowner to get his double-barrel shotgun if necessary. He had the choice of going to the visitor to talk or calling the dogs off and inviting the visitor in.

In our modern society, there is a constant flow of distressing information and obnoxious people having access to us and to our families without our permission. We can only react for there is no time to assess the situation and certainly no time to prepare for it. There is no way to keep the stress at bay when a television, a computer or a telephone can let the influence of any strangers inside the house before we have time to make a wise choice about whether or not to allow their input.

The Goat

We had a goat that served the purpose of guarding the property for a while. A beautiful car pulled into the yard one summer day with kinfolks coming to visit from Chicago. Aunt Ellie's daughter, Mary Jane, was bringing her new husband to be introduced to the relatives. Without dogs to alert us, we did not know right away that they had arrived. When we heard yelling, we looked outside to see that our goat had hopped onto the hood of their new car and was staring at them through the windshield. They were being held prisoner and were too afraid to get out of the car. We went to their rescue

Mabel Margaret Motes Bufford

immediately and removed the goat from their car. We didn't think to examine the car for damages, but the stranger, Mary Jane's husband, was probably assessing the damage while we greeted the children and hugged his wife. Our visitors were obviously afraid of the goat, so Mama told Joe and Andrew to tie the goat to a cedar tree in the front yard. As soon as it was safe, Mary Jane and her husband walked to the house. Within thirty minutes, Joe came in to inform Mama, "The goat is loose. He chewed through the rope."

"Get a chain and chain him to the cedar tree," Mama instructed Joe. The chain was found, and the goat was restrained. It wasn't long until Joe was back in the house again to report on the situation.

"The goat is trying to chew the cedar tree down now," he said.

"Just unchain him and let him go," Mama said in exasperation. She felt annoyed with the goat most of the time, but my siblings and I thought he was great fun, for he had personality and was a delightful playmate. He liked to play by chasing us around and around the house. We never ran so fast as when we looked back and saw him right on our heels. We feared that he would trample us if we were to fall, but he didn't. He was so sure footed that he could stop suddenly or he would jump over a child who fell and then stop to wait for them to get up and run again. One day when the goat was about to catch me, I darted inside the house and let the screen door slam behind me. I was laughing and thinking I had outsmarted the goat. Just as I turned to look back, the goat ran through the screen door to get to me. He wouldn't let anyone outdo him.

Going Hunting

Daddy got his gun out one afternoon to go hunting, and he planned to take Joe and Andrew. My sisters and I fussed because we were never invited to go hunting. "Awh, I rec'en you can go," Daddy said, "but you have to walk behind me and keep quiet." Daddy was leading the way with a rifle on his shoulder and had it pointed upward. The boys walked behind Daddy, and the girls brought up the rear. My sisters and I were delighted to be included.

"What a sight," Mama said to herself as she paused to watch her family march into the woods single file with the girls wearing little dresses.

Before we could get out of sight, the goat noticed we were leaving without him, and he ran to catch up. He did not fall in line, for he was not content to follow. He went directly to the front of the line and walked ahead of Daddy, who was the leader of this expedition. What nerve of him! He didn't know that we were "goin' huntin'," and he had not heard the rules about following where Daddy leads. Soon, Daddy made a right turn, and all of us turned as he had done. The goat was unaware that we had turned while he kept walking forward through the woods. When the goat finally noticed that we were no longer behind him, he ran to catch up. We thought he would fall in line at the rear so he would know the next time we made a turn. But he went straight to the head of the line again. Before long, we had forgotten about hunting. We spent the remainder of the outing trying to outsmart the goat and lose him in the woods. With all the noise we made, Daddy didn't get to see a thing to shoot at—though he was probably tempted to shoot the goat.

The goat was at home alone one day when we went away to visit our grandmother. We were not careful to lock the doors. When we returned, we found the goat had spent the day inside the house. We had no idea he would force the door open. There was incriminating evidence everywhere the goat had walked. Goat droppings were on top of the kitchen table and on the beds. Mama was furious and made it known that the goat would no longer be tolerated at our house. Daddy assured her he would take the goat to the sale barn the next day and sell him. Our memory of owning a pet goat was marred by having to help clean up the terrible mess he left behind. We hoped his next home had lots of children and locks on the doors.

Free Kittens

On rainy days, we could sit in the pickup truck which was left parked at the bus stop; its doors were never locked. It was crowded though, with all five of us, especially with our books. One day upon arriving at the bus stop, we were thrilled to discover that someone had dropped off several unwanted kittens. We played with the kittens until we saw the school bus coming, and then we placed them inside the truck to make sure they would still be there at the end of the long day. After school, we got off the bus and ran to the truck to retrieve the desperately hungry kittens. Mama was too amused to be angry when she saw her delighted children marching home smiling from ear to ear and each carrying a kitten. We neglected to give consideration to Daddy's reaction when he would discover the condition of his truck seat.

Marching to the Bus Stop

During deer hunting season, we feared being shot by hunters who might be unfamiliar with the area and would not expect us to be there, so we sang hymns loudly as we marched through the woods to the bus stop. With the noise we made, there probably was not a deer within a mile of us.

We knew to expect carelessness from hunters, because we had been working in the cotton field once when bullets struck the ground near us. We assumed it was not intentional since no more shots were fired after we began to yell. We concluded that it might have been our neighbor, Johnny Bryant, shooting at blackbirds on the adjoining property and not expecting us to be in the field.

The first year we owned turkeys, Mama and Daddy made plans to kill a turkey and cook it while their children picked cotton on Thanksgiving morning. With great excitement, we left for the field to fill our pick sacks as quickly as possible. This would be our family's first Thanksgiving dinner. All morning, I looked forward to seeing a beautiful brown turkey on the table in a big platter just like in the pictures I saw at school. When we came in to eat at noon, I looked about in the kitchen for the turkey on a platter. It was such a disappointment when I asked to see the turkey and my mother pointed to a big soup pot on the woodstove with cut-up, boiled turkey meat in it.

Freezing at the Bus Stop

My sisters and I were as skinny as a rail and wore cotton dresses even in the winter. We were often cold, though we wore long coats. Rayon headscarves tied under the chin kept the wind out of our ears. When the temperature was in the teens or lower, Daddy would go to the bus stop ahead of us and build a fire in a metal barrel so we could hover around it and warm our hands. Most of the time, we had gloves, but during the times that we didn't, we could carry hot baked sweet potatoes in our pockets that had been left from breakfast. We enjoyed getting to eat sweet potatoes while waiting for the school bus.

Eventually, Daddy built a shed at the bus stop so we could be protected from the cold wind while we waited for the

Walking with God in the Backwoods

school bus. He had salvaged some of the padded theater seats that the church gave away and placed them inside so we could sit in comfort. The shed also gave us a place to store our boots until we got back from school and changed into them for wading through the slough.

—⧖—

High Heels

While walking one summer day, we found a "junk pile" in the edge of the woods where someone had discarded their unwanted items. My sisters and I could hardly believe our good fortune in having found several pairs of old high-heel shoes. We clomped around in those high heels until we had blisters on our feet. We left the assortment of high heels in the shed at the main road so we could switch shoes after Sunday school to walk through the moist slough. We would walk to the house in the high heels mostly because we enjoyed it so much and partly to prolong the life of our good church shoes which we carried.

Two of Uncle Jesse's daughters, Olivee and Thelma, were invited to stay overnight with us when their family visited us one Saturday. It was a delightful treat for us that did not happen often. They enjoyed putting on a pair of the high heels and walking with our family through the woods from the house to the truck on Sunday morning. It was miserable to ride inside our truck when the small children sat on our lap.

For that reason, my parents were easily persuaded to let the older children ride in the back of the truck on this particular Sunday. We thoroughly enjoyed the four-mile ride to church as the wind blew against our faces and tousled our hair. It was not unusual to see a big family packed into a pickup truck and the little children standing with their angelic faces near the windshield.

The Rickshaw

On Sunday afternoon, we played with an unusual toy Daddy had made for us out of two big metal wheels attached to an axle. He probably got it free from his friend's junkyard. Daddy always watched for free stuff to bring home, and he'd make some interesting things out of it. Daddy built a flatbed between the wheels that could be raised or lowered like a seesaw by the long handles attached to the front. One older child could walk about holding on to both handles and give rides to the younger children like a rickshaw. We were the envy of our visitors for it was great fun but very dangerous. It was impossible to stay on the flatbed if the person pulling the rickshaw turned loose of the handles and let them fly upward. It is amazing that we managed to get through our whole childhood without anyone having broken bones.

Walking in Darkness

Mama had long ago given up church attendance in the evening because of a bad memory of a hazardous walk across a footbridge in the darkness on the way home. One time when she was carrying Kathy in her arms, she and the baby fell into the shallow water. Olivee, Thelma, Audrey, and I were eager to go to the Sunday evening service with Daddy knowing we would have to walk through the woods in the darkness on the way back after church. The girls and I donned a pair of ragged high heels as we headed off to the truck again which was parked at the main road.

By the time we left the evening church service, it was starting to get dark. Daddy pulled off the main road and parked the pickup truck. All the girls rushed to the shed and eagerly put the high heels on again. We marched single file with Daddy leading the way and carrying a kerosene lantern. It became very dark as we went deep into the woods, and the well-worn path seemed especially narrow since grass and vegetation had begun to overtake it. What was fun in the daylight was scary at night. I brought up the rear so the visitors could be closer to our fearless leader and to the source of light as all the girls struggled to walk in high heels while keeping up with him. I hoped there were no snakes where I was placing my feet in the darkness. In Arkansas, everyone lived with an awareness of poisonous snakes. We were regularly warned about copperheads, cottonmouths, water moccasins, and rattlesnakes.

"Is there likely to be snakes out here?" I heard Olivee asking my father.

"Naw," he assured her, "with me uh stompin', it'll scare 'em away. 'Sides, snakes are more skreed of us than we are of them." I needed to hear those reassuring words from Daddy as much as Olivee did. I did not say a word, for I wanted everyone to think I was very brave as I walked in the darkness. I was so relieved to see the dim glow of light up ahead coming from the kerosene lamps that were shining through the windows of home. I was feeling more courage by the moment. As we approached the porch in single file, I could not resist the urge to play a trick on Olivee. I rushed forward as she lifted one leg to step onto the porch, and I pinched the back of her other bare leg, just above the heel. When my sharp fingernails touched her leg, she shrieked in terror while making her final lunge onto the porch. Had I not doubled over with laughter, she would have died of fright thinking that she had been bitten by a venomous snake.

<blockquote>
Thy word is a lamp unto my feet
and a light unto my path.

—Psalms 119:105
</blockquote>

Where Could I Go but to the Lord
Easter Sunday, 1960

WE DIDN'T GO VERY MANY places—mostly school and church. Since we had few toys, we often played house or played school, and sometimes, we even played church. Fortunately, our little brothers and sisters were compliant and served happily as the attentive congregation. Each of the older children enjoyed getting a chance to be the mother, the teacher, or the preacher.

On Easter Sunday, we went to spend the day at Uncle Jesse's house near Tuckerman, at a place called Denton Island. It wasn't really an island; it was just a few miles of higher ground located in the bottoms. Half of Uncle Jesse and Aunt Veelia's fourteen children still lived at home. Two of their younger children, Johnny and Genice, had been slightly crippled by the polio they contracted in 1952.

We arrived in an older black car that would soon be sold as junk iron. I was riding in the backseat next to the window, but I could hardly see out. My mother had placed little dresses on hangers over the window, and they blocked my view. She was pleased with the homemade dresses she had made for her youngest child, Kathy, who was near four years old. Having felt ambitious and creative, Mama sewed all during the long winter and was eager to show her handiwork to the ladies.

As the car came to a halt in Uncle Jesse's driveway, relatives stepped off the front porch and walked toward our car to welcome us. Their home was the favorite place for family gatherings. My fourteen-year-old cousin, Olivee, stepped to the car door, saying, "Howdy, howdy, howdy." Her boldness seemed strange to me, for all the children in my family were painfully shy.

For Southern folks, dinner was the noon meal. The evening meal was always called supper. Aunt Veelia had made a large meal with fried potatoes, corn bread, and a big pot of vegetable soup. On that Easter Sunday, a much larger number of relatives had arrived than there were dishes and silverware in the kitchen. Plates and cups made of paper or Styrofoam were a luxury that poor farm laborers could not afford. We went to the kitchen, formed a disorganized line, and filled our plates. The older folks ate in the kitchen while the younger people carried their plates to the living room or to the porch to find a place to sit while eating. I was eating in the living room when I noticed that Edna, one of Uncle Jesse's married daughters, was eating from a bread pan, with a large stirring spoon, and drinking iced tea from a canning jar. I pointed it out to the others sitting nearby, and we all had a good laugh.

—ᴍ—

Church in the Barn

After dinner, a dozen children of various ages went to the big barn to climb around and to explore. Olivee suggested that we should have church, and she would be the preacher. Everyone was in agreement. It was more enjoyable to play church when a daring person would consent to preach. While she fetched song books and a bible, we found a comfortable place to sit. We were just as serious as if we were in a real church service. With boldness, Olivee led us in singing several lively hymns that were familiar to everyone. We weren't just playing church, we were "havin' church." Then, Olivee opened her bible to begin the sermon. I can't recall exactly which scripture passage she chose to read, but I do remember it was from the book of Revelations and it was about weird creatures.

After hearing several verses, I noticed a tingling sensation on the back of my head that affected the scalp from ear to ear; it was not painful, but unusual. The other children seemed to be unaffected. They were oblivious to my predicament, for their attention was riveted on Olivee, the youthful speaker. I moved my head slowly up and down and from side to side, hoping the strange feeling would go away. The sensation seemed to be spreading toward the crown of my head.

I should get out of here, I thought. *This is scaring me.*

About halfway to the farmhouse, I heard a voice inside my spirit—similar to what one would know as the conscience. The voice was not loud, and by the time I had slowed my pace so I could concentrate on hearing it, the unusual communication of words had ended. It was as much perceived as it was heard. I sensed that God was singling me out for a purpose and would require something of me. Though I cannot recall the exact words, I understood that God has a plan for my life, and I have been chosen for a special assignment.

I knew it was God. I did not look around for another explanation for the words I'd heard; there was no need. Though I had heard the Bible story about God talking to Samuel as a lad, I had not been told to expect that God would talk to me. I felt compelled to answer Him. In a manner typical of an eleven-year-old with bad grammar, I answered God, "Just don't make me no preacher."

I was no longer aware of the skin-crawling sensation as I walked to the house, but the presence of God was still around me as I stepped onto the porch. I opened the screen door and entered. Several ladies were sitting about in the living room, relaxing and talking. Their conversation was about a sensitive matter, which caused me to have a feeling of disgust. Not that the words they said were bad, but human words did not fare

Walking with God in the Backwoods

well in contrast to words spoken directly from God. I was experiencing an altered sense of consciousness with all my senses on high alert. The heightened sense of awareness made me feel more alive or at least more aware of being alive. I continued to walk through the living room without speaking to anyone, and they did not speak to me. Each sensation and impression was being permanently recorded in my memory. I walked into the kitchen where the unwashed dishes were still on the table in disarray. An outdoor cat had crept inside the house and was on the table sniffing the leftovers. Though I knew it was unacceptable for the cat to be inside, I made no effort to remove him. I walked straight through the kitchen and out the backdoor. I have no memory of the visit beyond that point. The heavy presence of God had lifted; I was back to normal, and everything became ordinary again.

Many years went by before I mentioned the experience to anyone. I finally told my younger brother, Joe, and he remembered the Spirit-filled, church service in the barn. Joe said, "After you left, some kids b'gin speakin' in tongues." His first impulse was to go to the house and *tell*.

Joe Goes to Tell

A mother with a large amount of children often found it helpful to have a child in the family who played the role of the informer. In that way, the mother could know everything that went on while her children were out of her sight. Though it might be a convenient alliance for the mother, it was often harmful to the child. While the tattling child was rewarded with approval from their grateful mother, they suffered a diminished relationship with their siblings.

Nine-year-old Joe went to the house on that occasion to tell Mama what was going on in the barn. Of course, Mama was very interested. When Joe opened his mouth to tell her, he began to speak in tongues and had no ability to stop himself. When he could not speak English, he turned in astonishment and walked away. Having experienced the outpouring of the Holy Spirit at Weona Junction, Mama recognized what was happening. "It's the Holy Ghost," she said with amazement as she looked toward the other ladies. Aunt Veelia smiled knowingly with a twinkle in her eyes.

The Lord God must have enjoyed the children who were in one mind and one accord as they worshiped Him in the barn that day. I think God was answering another prayer for our grandmother, Mary. I know that is a possibility because every believing mother prays not only for the salvation of her children but for the salvation of her grandchildren. This was the second time when several Motes family members were united in love and unity, one mind and one accord, and had a supernatural experience. It seemed that God's Holy Spirit hovered close by for many months to give us strength and comfort for the dark days ahead.

Times Are Changing

As little girls, Audrey and I were very near the same size and were sometimes asked if we were twins. We were constant companions by day and shared the same bed at night. We were inseparable. The summer before, we had gone walking after breakfast each morning side by side with both of us having one arm around the other's shoulder. Barefoot, we walked aimlessly along the outline of the lawn on a little dirt road that Daddy had plowed to separate the yard from the cotton field. It was great fun for both of us to take a turn telling our dreams while they were still fresh on our mind.

The turns and twists of our dreams were as bizarre as any science fiction movie and very entertaining. It was just as entertaining for us to tell our dreams as it was for children in other families to watch cartoons on television. It certainly made us more aware of our dreams as we recalled the details and recited them in the early hours of the morning. But that was a child's game that we had outgrown and we would not play it again.

I was eleven years old in the spring of 1960, and Audrey was twelve and a half. We were changing and growing up. I was having private thoughts that I didn't share with anyone. There were things to ponder, like the little church service in the barn and the conversation with God afterward. Such thoughts could only be trusted to the Lord. Audrey was becoming an extremely private person too, and there was a wider divide coming between us. She was far more mature than her years as a result of the responsibilities that she carried. Because Audrey was capable and so willing to work around the house, Mama counted on her more every year.

Housework was an activity I did not enjoy sharing with Audrey. The more work she chose to do, the less I would be asked to do. I remember being concerned that if I should venture to learn a new skill, it would become my duty to perform it from that day forth. I admired Audrey's homemaking skills and felt bad about my lack when I compared myself to her. I was lazy, and among the old folks, that was one of the worst things you could say about a person. The next worst thing to being a lazy person was being a "no account." Of course, there were worst levels of evil beyond that. Every person was supposed to have a skill or a talent to bring to the table for the benefit of the family. The only job I really enjoyed was that of rocking the baby to sleep after supper each night. After Mama finished the dishes, she would find that I had not only gotten the baby to sleep but I had fallen into a deep sleep as well. Needless to say, I was a late bloomer and couldn't imagine why God would choose me for any purpose, especially when Audrey was available.

Planting Corn

All the children in our family, including four-year-old Kathy, were incorporated to help plant four rows of corn in a long, seventeen-acre field alongside the cotton. Daddy plowed a furrow with his tractor and cultivator as his children walked along behind dropping a couple kernels of corn about every twelve inches. At the end of the day, I overheard Daddy telling Mama about Kathy dropping several kernels of corn in each hill. They were both amused at her efforts. I sensed they had much delight in her.

At the end of a long day of work, Daddy placed some hand tools on the porch and sat down on the edge to rest. Gathering around him, several of us sat with our skinny legs dangling off the edge of the porch. While Kathy walked along behind those who were seated, she curiously picked up a hammer and pecked Joe on the head with it lightly. It was not hard enough to inflict great pain, but Daddy's response was quick. He jerked the dusty cap off his head and began "frailing" Kathy over the head with it. His fury was like that of a setting hen flogging an intruder. There had been no malice on Kathy's part—just a desire to play with the hammer and to include her brother. She loved her brother and wanted his attention. Kathy learned a quick lesson, but the lesson was not lost on the rest of us. We learned that we should walk softly around our father lest we step across an unseen boundary and incur his wrath.

Mabel Margaret Motes Bufford

Though our father was very good in so many ways, he did not talk to us often individually. We were not always told where the boundaries were; we only knew that if we should step over an invisible line, punishment would be swift, harsh, and often humiliating. We learned to walk softly, subconsciously discerning his moods to avoid a mistake which would result in an unpleasant experience. Though there were few times that we saw his wrath, those times were memorable. To be singled out usually meant punishment was to be administered or instructions given for a job assignment, and I disliked both intensely.

> Even a child is known by his doings,
> whether his work be pure, and whether it be right.
>
> —Proverbs 20:11

No Tears in Heaven
1960

ON A MISERABLY HUMID SUMMER day in 1960, I walked aimlessly to the front screen door to look outside at nothing in particular. Our old black car was parked in the yard some distance away, under the oak tree. The car was a Buick and similar to the cars that the Chicago gangsters drove. For a second, I thought it looked like a funeral hearse. In amazement, I turned to my mother who was sewing nearby and told her with a chuckle what I had seen, or what I thought I had seen. She looked up briefly and then went on with her work without a comment. Seeing something for a second that is not really there would happen again a couple times in my life before I would learn to question the Lord about its meaning.

Mama had suffered from a fear of death much of her adult life. It became worse when she was feeling ill. She often worried that she might die and leave a house full of little children for my dad to bring up. Occasionally, she would annoy us with her melancholy mood.

"You should be thankful for me," she said with a nagging tone. "If I wuz to die, you'd have to be raised by a *stepmother*." The way she stressed the word *step* we knew we wouldn't want a stepmother. On that particular day, Mama was especially depressed. "Sometimes, I think I won't live to be fifty-six years old." Audrey had heard all she could stand of those dismal comments.

"So what," Audrey responded harshly, "sometimes, I think I won't live to be thirty-four." Mama never talked in such a gloomy manner again. She lived much of her life in silence.

I've often wondered what made Audrey have thoughts about dying before the age of thirty-four. Had God communicated information to her about the future? I wonder if she had an experience with God when the children had church in the barn and if the Lord spoke to her similar to the way He spoke to me. No one questioned Audrey about her comment. Her sharp reply was meant to close that conversation, and it surely did just that.

My First Prophetic Dream

That same summer, at eleven years old, I had the first prophetic dream that I was aware of, and I too chose not tell anyone of it. In the vivid dream, which lasted only a few seconds, I was holding the limp body of my youngest sister, Kathy, as she lay draped across my arms. Though Kathy was a healthy, normal four-year-old, in my dream, she was dead. It was simply a fact, and there was no sense of grief. In the dream, Audrey was standing at my side, but I was the one holding the dead child in my arms. In real life, I would not be the mature, responsible one for I was always in Audrey's shadow. In the dream, I looked in the distance, and there were enemy soldiers coming toward us in the woods at the far end of the cotton field. There might have been as many as three infantrymen that I could see clearly moving toward us like commandos darting from tree to tree. I sensed that there were several more that were unseen. I had a sense of urgency and perceived that the armed soldiers were coming for Kathy—not for me and not for Audrey. *I must hide her*, I thought as I whirled around and ran with the dead child in my arms. Audrey ran behind me as we rushed through the backyard and into the vegetable garden where I dug a grave quickly. There was no explanation for how we had obtained a shovel. It just appeared. Within seconds of digging, we placed Kathy in the grave and covered her with dirt. I looked up to find that the approaching soldiers were gone. I wiped my brow with a sigh of relief, thinking, *She's safe.* The troubling dream ended, leaving me with more to ponder. Several years passed before I realized the many things God was telling me in that short prophetic dream.

The Family Portrait at the Zoo

On August 29, 1960, my older brother, Mike, was kind enough to drive us to visit the zoo in Memphis, Tennessee. It was to be our first visit to a zoo and our first visit to the big city. In the hustle and bustle of getting loaded up, my six-year-old brother, Andrew, screamed out—his finger had been slammed in the car door. My heart ached for him as my

Walking with God in the Backwoods

parents rushed to examine his fingers. No bones were broken, so we continued our day trip. Even Andrew's throbbing finger could not eliminate his enthusiasm for an outing to the faraway zoo.

Everything in the city was new to us—the sights, the sounds, and the smells—and we felt an eagerness to take it all in. We enjoyed observing the exotic animals that we had seen only in picture books at school. Most of all, we enjoyed the monkeys whose wacky antics made us desire one for a house pet.

Near the exit gate at the zoo, a photographer called out from his booth to those who passed by encouraging them to have their picture taken. It had been a desire of my mothers' heart to have a portrait of her family, but she had dismissed the idea because the chances of it happening were improbable. We rarely went into a town large enough to have a photographer's studio. The expense, the planning, and the preparation for an event such as an appointment with a photographer would have been beyond my family's means and ability to implement. Mama was eager to take advantage of the opportunity to have a family portrait taken quickly and easily at such an unexpected time and place. The picture was not of highest quality, but it only cost about three dollars. Mama tried to get Mike to join us, but typical of a college student, he chose not to be in the photograph with the unrefined group. Knowing that we did not own a camera and had little chance of ever "having our picture made," Mike waited patiently for us while we took advantage of our golden moment. The photo was mailed to our address a week or two later.

Picking Cotton

The new school term began after the Labor Day holiday. That gave poor kids a chance to pick cotton for a week or two before school started and during the holiday. We received money for the cotton we picked in our father's fields when he got paid for the wagon load of cotton that he took to the Newport cotton gin. The rate of pay was about three dollars for a hundred pounds of cotton. It took all day for me to pick one hundred pounds of cotton; therefore, the most I made was three dollars a day. We learned how to pick cotton using both hands at the same time but did not develop much speed. The children in my family worked more carefully than other people so we wouldn't be hurt by the sharp points on the cotton boll. We picked only one row at a time and managed to keep up with other field hands who were picking two rows. We used a shorter pick sack, no more than seven feet in length, because we would not be able to lift a sack which was nine feet long and filled with cotton.

A really good cotton picker could pick two hundred pounds or more a day and earn six dollars. Often, those people had sore fingers that were bloodied by the sharp points of

Walking with God in the Backwoods

the cotton bolls. Only the better cotton pickers dragged their longer sack between two rows and picked both rows. After working in a bent over position for several minutes, it became extremely painful to rise to an upright position. Often, the cotton sacks were packed down until they were stiff and hard to drag. It took a strong person to lift a full sack of cotton over their shoulder and carry it to the end of the field. Daddy often carried the heavy sacks of cotton for the womenfolk and lifted their sacks onto the scale. While Daddy announced the weight of the cotton, Mama recorded the number of pounds in a little booklet provided by the cotton gin. There were usually young men who volunteered to climb into the cotton wagon to empty the cotton sacks which Daddy lifted up to them.

Six- to ten-year-old children were given a tow sack or burlap bag with a fabric strap, and they picked cotton along with their parents. A child of three to five years old often carried a pillow case to occupy themselves picking a little bit of cotton near their mothers. A mother's sack cushioned with cotton provided a place where a young child could nap. Fieldwork was very hard on mothers who had experienced numerous pregnancies and physical problems related to child bearing.

In my parents' day, people used the word *folks* often. In addition to white folks and black folks, there were women and men folks, young and old folks, and rich and poor folks.

Occasionally, we picked cotton with black folk from Weiner who wanted to make a little extra money working in our fields. It was different working with black people than when only white people were in the field. The black people joked as they worked and laughed loudly. They yelled to their friends who were quite a distance away and had a good time while they worked. They made the job more pleasant, and the day went by much more quickly.

The white folk seemed to be more serious and subdued. They would often carry on a conversation only with those who worked nearby. However, they did laugh and joke with others while at the truck having their cotton weighed and their pick sack emptied.

I was aware that the children in my family were spoiled for we were not punished if we did not work hard enough. We sometimes worked with young children from other poor families who were threatened by their parents with a whoopin' at the end of the day if they did not pick a certain amount of cotton. People only picked cotton when they had no other way to earn the money they needed. It was certainly a hard way to earn a dollar.

Kathy Becomes Sick

Four-year-old Kathy had been feeling bad for a few days but was not really complaining; she just lay around more

Walking with God in the Backwoods

than was normal. On Saturday, October 1, 1960, we were picking cotton in a field we had rented from George Smith near Weiner. Seven-year-old Mildred babysat at the truck all day, caring for Andrew and Kathy while we older children picked cotton with Mama and Daddy. The truck was parked under a thorn tree and in the edge of the gravel road. It was a long, boring day for the little barefoot children who tried to avoid getting thorns in their feet. Kathy took a nap in the truck seat, and when she awoke, she tried to rise and could not get into a sitting position. She said to Mildred, "Go tell Mama that I can't walk." I can remember Mildred coming to the field to give Mama the message and how alarming it sounded to me. Mama took her pick sack off immediately, leaving it in the field and walked to the truck to check on Kathy. Audrey, Joe, and I kept working. Mildred said Mama held Kathy in her arms and walked around with her. When Kathy began vomiting, Mildred could not bear to watch and walked away. Daddy was responsible for all the hired hands who were working for us, and Mama couldn't drive, so we stayed a couple more hours until the workday was over. Kathy did not seem to be in pain and seemed to feel better after her stomach had settled.

The following morning, we did not go to Sunday school and church like we usually did. Daddy drove to Clark's general store to buy Kathy something special to eat or to drink. We were more likely to get a grocery item like orange juice or a soda pop if we were sick. Audrey and I were excited to go with Daddy to the store. We were fortunate to be taken along more often while our younger siblings were kept at home. I had about two dollars in my purse that I had earned picking cotton, and I wanted to buy Kathy a gift to cheer her up. There was a pair of white socks that were really pretty that were called poodle socks, and they felt bumpy or wavy to the touch. I bought them for Kathy, and she showed pleasure in receiving them as I put them on her feet. Mama told me to get Kathy dressed, and they would take her to see the doctor at the Newport hospital.

When I started to dress her, she began to whimper as if she was reluctant to go to the doctor. I said to her, "Oh, don't be afraid, that doctor is not going to kill you."

We were seldom left at home alone, and it felt strange. After a couple of hours, Mike arrived from Memphis and found that we were without supervision. He drove us to Grandma West's house where we left Joe, Mildred, and Andrew. Then, Mike took me and Audrey with him to find Mama, Daddy, and Kathy at the hospital. We had not been expecting Mike to visit us. How nice that the Lord had arranged for him to come to our house that afternoon.

When we arrived at the hospital, we found Kathy lying on a gurney that was parked in the hallway against the wall and our worried parents standing beside her. She had been examined by a doctor, and it was suspected that she needed an operation to remove her appendix. She was not fussing or showing emotion but lay very still and calmly looked at us

Walking with God in the Backwoods

as if she felt no pain. Audrey and I listened quietly as Mike talked to our parents and they gave him instructions as to the care of the children in their absence.

Audrey and I stood looking at Kathy but did not speak to her nor did she indicate that she had any desire to speak to us. She looked all right to me, except that she was very still and strangely silent.

—∿—

Day of Sadness

After leaving the hospital, Mike, Audrey, and I returned to our grandmother's house to let her know the situation and ask if we could stay a few days and pick cotton with her. We headed back to the farm to gather up pick sacks for each of the five school children. Mike parked his nice 1958 Chevrolet at the county road, and we began to walk through the woods toward the house. The ground was suitably dry, but Mike did not want to drive his new car through the woods and risk having it scratched by low-hanging tree limbs. It had been little more than two hours since we left the hospital, and our closest neighbors saw us as we drove passed their house and slowed to turn in at our property.

A short time before, the Trotter family had received a grim message by phone from the hospital to be given to Mike, and they began watching for his car. As we walked along, we could hear a male voice urgently yelling Mike's name in the distance. Since the voice came from behind us, Mike said he would go back and see what the neighbor wanted. He told Audrey and me to go on to the house and get our picks sacks and meet him back at the car.

When Audrey and I got back to the car with the pick sacks and a few extra items, Mike waited for us to get seated inside the car before he told us the message our neighbor, Larry Trotter, had given to him: "Kathy is dead. She died on the operating table." Audrey began to cry softly, but I sat in stunned silence as if numb and unable to respond. Mike was grim and did not show much emotion either. While we were sitting in the car, James and Zelza Easter stopped to tell us the message in case we had not yet heard the devastating news. Mike told them that the Trotter family had given him the message. It must have been about 5:30 p.m. when the Easter family was on their way to church for the evening service that would start at 6:00 p.m. As Mike started the car and began to drive away, he quoted a scripture from the book of Job: "The Lord gave, and the Lord hath taken away; blessed be the name of the Lord."

Mike took Audrey and me to Grandma's where all were gathered in the dining room and told Grandma and our younger siblings the sad news. Grandma began to cry right away, but Joe, Mildred, and Andrew were stunned just as I had been. My body and mind must have gone into a degree of shock, for I tried to remember Kathy, but I could not picture her in my mind though I had just seen her and that worried

Walking with God in the Backwoods

me. Remembering the last words I had said to her filled me with regret that I had not been gentle, kind, and loving.

Daddy brought Mama from the hospital to Grandma's so we could all be together.

After a short time, he took Uncle John Horace West with him to go to Uncle Jesse's house to inform their family for Grandma and our closest relatives had no phones. Mike drove back to Memphis to make arrangements to take time off work for Kathy's funeral.

Mama told us the nurse started to take the new socks off Kathy's feet when it was time for her to go into surgery, but she indicated by pulling her foot away that she wanted to keep the pretty socks on her feet. When Mama and Daddy prayed for Kathy and said good-bye before she was taken into surgery, she was calm and pleased to be wearing the new socks. Mama told us that upon being informed that Kathy had passed away, the doctor ordered a sedative for her and had her to lie down while a nurse helped Daddy by making phone calls to our closest neighbor, the Trotter family. The Easter family was called so they could pass the message at our church. God had been merciful to Kathy for He took her away very gently. The socks were probably removed after the anesthetic was administered, for they were presented to Mama immediately after Kathy's death.

Kathy had gone barefoot all summer, and my mother had just recently bought a pair of rubbery flip-flops for her to wear to church. In the winter months, she had worn shoes handed down from Andrew. Since she was too young to attend school, she did not require new shoes. At four years old, Kathy had lived and died without ever having a pair of pretty new shoes of her own.

—ᴍ—

Kathy's Funeral

Mike return from Memphis the next day and drove us to Newport so we could make funeral arrangements. When Daddy was asked for information for the obituary, he was still so affected by shock and grief that he could not recite all his children's names without help from Mama. Mike took us to a store and bought a black dress for Mama and a black hat with a veil black gloves and shoes for her to wear. He also bought a few items of nice clothing for his brothers and sisters to wear to the funeral. Mama picked out a pretty pink and white dress for Kathy to wear in her casket. It was probably the only new store-bought dress she ever wore.

Some of Mama's relatives from Pitts came and cleaned our house and did acts of kindness to show their love and to ease our pain. We did not use our house to receive mourners, for it would be unhandy for people to walk through the woods. Those who grieved with us gathered at the funeral home where there was electricity, air conditioning, a flush toilet, and tissue. One of the things we appreciated most was that Dorothy Walker took photographs and gave them to us later.

Walking with God in the Backwoods

Some details we would not have remembered if there had not been photographs taken. Because we were not inclined to be social people, my siblings and I were out of our comfort zone at the viewing and funeral where we functioned as if in a dream.

—m—

Aunt Ellie

Someone in Uncle Jesse's family had contacted Aunt Ellie in Chicago, and she immediately arranged to take off work and bought a bus ticket to Newport to attend the funeral. When it was time for the funeral procession to leave the funeral home and drive to the Harmony Grove church for the funeral, Aunt Ellie still had not arrived. As the long string of cars headed down Highway 14, with a police escort, all oncoming traffic pulled over and stopped to show their respect. Among the many people in cars waiting patiently for us to go passed, we saw a big Greyhound bus with the driver standing in front of it waving. Behind the bus, a woman was standing in the street with her suitcase and waving as if to flag us down. Right away, my father recognized her and exclaimed, "There's Ellie!" Looking backward as we passed her, my Father said, "Jesse is back there. He'll get her." Uncle Jesse was bringing up the rear of the funeral procession and easily pulled over to provide transportation for Aunt Ellie. We were so happy to see her as we organized to walk inside the church. Aunt Ellie stayed beside my mother and gave my parents emotional support.

When I stepped inside the church, I saw that the back rows of pews were full for the first time. Seated on the left side of the church, about halfway down the pew, was Larry Trotter. He was turned in his seat so he could see us as we came in. He and I made eye contact, and then I lowered my gaze. It was a weekday, and Larry had missed school to be at Kathy's funeral. I knew he felt more than the usual feelings of sympathy. Having been emotionally involved, he was greatly affected by the death of his little neighbor.

As we filed passed the little blue casket for the last time and headed out of the church, I looked back and found that Daddy was holding Mama's hand as the two of them exited the church. That was nice and something special that I had never seen them do before. Mama and Daddy were not ones to show affection and did not allow the girls and boys to touch each other after the age of ten.

Aunt Ellie was so gracious to stay with us for a few days. She had Daddy to drive her to Weiner where she bought fabric and sewing supplies for us so we could make new dresses. It was more than a thoughtful idea; it showed the gift of wisdom for it was a gift that kept on giving. We needed something exciting like new dresses to look forward to and a sewing project to fill our spare time in the coming winter months. It was like therapy for Mama, Audrey, Mildred, and me in our time of grief. My mother did not always have

Walking with God in the Backwoods

nice fabric for sewing, and it was a gift that was very much appreciated in our family. Aunt Ellie's love and concern was very comforting. Even more than her gifts, we appreciated her presence. She made a difference.

It was very difficult for my parents to deal with Kathy's sudden death. I'm sure they had moments when they wondered, *How could our Heavenly Father have allowed this to happen in our family?* If they did, I was not aware of it.

My mother mentioned Kathy's name almost every day for the first year after the funeral. I think she feared that we might forget Kathy if she didn't keep her memory alive. Mama would occasionally tell us a memory she had of Kathy and enjoyed hearing the memories of others as well.

Mama told us about arriving at Harmony Grove church nearly an hour before the service was to start, in the late summer of 1960. Geraldine Keller arrived early with her parents, and Noel Madison and Pastor James Bittle arrived early as well. Noel and Geraldine sat on one side of the sanctuary to be alone and talked softly for this was their special time together. While my parents talked to others, my mother was watching Kathy from a short distance. As Kathy wandered near the young couple, Mama was prepared to call for her if it appeared that her presence was an intrusion. As my mother observed, Noel offered Geraldine a piece of gum and then gave a piece of gum to Kathy. It was a rare treat for Kathy, a child in poverty, to get a piece of chewing gum. With delight, Kathy returned to Mama's side to enjoy her good fortune. It might have been just one piece of gum and it might have happened only once, but it was no small kindness to my mother.

As the ultimate good parent, our Heavenly Father hovers over His little ones to observe what they do and what is done to them. He is certainly no less caring and attentive than the best earthy mother. Not only does He take note but He also keeps a record, and He gives rewards for good behavior. God gives rewards to those who *give*. If we want a reward in this life, we should be a giver, for Jesus said, "That thy alms may be in secret: and thy Father which seeth in secret himself shall reward thee openly" (Matt. 6:4).

A famous English researcher, Dr. Jane Goodall, said, "You cannot get through a single day without having an impact on the world around you." I questioned that statement until I remembered how Noel had endeared himself to my mother with such a simple act of kindness to her little child. It was such an inconsequential act that Noel says he has no memory of it. Even our smallest actions create a memory and leave behind an impression. In the Bible, we are told that if we give even a cup of cold water in the name of Jesus, we'll receive a reward (see Matt. 10:42). A reward for something this little, we might ask? I've discovered that it isn't how big or costly the gifts happens to be, God rewards those who give. "Give and it shall be given unto you" (Luke 6:38).

There were dark days when the emotion of grief battered my parents like ocean waves, but they simply "carried on."

Their faith was anchored in God's goodness, and that gave them hope for the future. They became even more faithful to God and more committed to church attendance than ever before. My parents had the same attitude that Job had: "Though he slay me, yet will I trust in him: but I will maintain mine own ways before him" (Job 13:15). As children, my siblings and I became more serious and introverted. We fought less and appreciated one another more. Knowing that death could come to anyone at any time caused us to take life more seriously.

> For this God is our God for ever and ever:
> he will be our guide even unto death.

> —Psalms 48:14

Hold to God's Unchanging Hand
1961

IN THE EARLY SPRING, THE Arkansas landscape came to life, just in time to celebrate the resurrection of Christ on Easter Sunday. Spring arrived with a burst of joy and surrounded us with the beauty of nature. The woods were full of flowering dogwoods blooming against the drab background of trees just waking from winter solstice. The splendor of redbud trees in bloom offered a vivid splash of color in the woods nearby. Four large peach trees along the side of the house produced a glorious display of pink blossoms that looked like a little bit of heaven on earth. Spring was Mama's favorite season, and she loved the crocus and daffodils that burst into bloom to rejoice with her. The turtles came out of seclusion to sunbathe on logs half submerged in the muddy water in the slough while the voices of a thousand croaking frogs announced a new beginning. The sounds in nature were as music to her ears.

Pans of water from washing and rinsing the dishes were eagerly carried by Mama to the yard to be poured around the flowers. Going outside put variety in her housework routine, and she appreciated the refreshing break to visit such beauty. Nature was Mama's sanctuary where she communed with the Lord. At times like this, she was truly happy.

Living Off the Land

Most families like ours who sharecropped or worked in the timber were desperately poor. Out of necessity we lived off the land as much as possible. Living off the land is not as easy as it sounds because everything that is edible in the country might be miles apart, and it has a ripening season of short duration. While hunting for small game, other hunters also watched for small fruit-bearing trees called persimmon, mulberry, and muscadine from which excellent jam and jelly could be made. When there were other families in need, the ripened fruit was taken quickly by the one who arrived first.

Mama was very resourceful and lived like a pioneer woman. She cooked wild poke salad which grew most often in road ditches and along a fence row. We gathered hickory nuts from the ground beneath a hickory tree. My brothers and sisters and I sat in the yard cracking the nuts between two rocks or by hitting them with a hammer. It was a tedious job to pick out the meaty portion of each nut with a pocket knife or a bobby pin.

Berry Picking

Wearing her sun bonnet, Mama eagerly organized my brothers and sisters and me to carry buckets for picking blackberries in the heat of summer. Sweating and complaining, we trudged through the thickets wearing wading boots. Swarming mosquitoes danced around our faces and attacked any uncovered skin they could find. Long sleeves that afforded some protection from the annoying mosquitoes became snagged immediately by the sharp briars. While picking berries, we risked being scratched, bloodied, and bitten. It was a miserable job, but our desire for fresh-baked blackberry cobbler gave us the necessary determination to press on.

Not only birds and small animals but snakes were also drawn to blackberry vines for a source of food. Small garter snakes were well hidden beneath leaves as they stretched out on the berry vines. The discovery of more and more luscious berries could almost make us forget to watch for snakes. It always brought a startled reaction when we extended our hand and almost touched a garter snake. The real danger was the poisonous snakes most likely to be at our feet.

A Woman's Work Is Never Done

Each summer, Mama canned vegetables and fruit by the bushels using a pressure canner on a wood cook stove. It was unbearably hot in the house, and we had no electricity for fans. Audrey and I sat under the shade tree in the front yard peeling juicy tomatoes or breaking green beans for hours at a time to prepare the fresh vegetables for canning. Mildred was often left alone in the kitchen to watch the pressure gauge on the pressure canner so Mama could go about her work outside the house. It was an especially miserable assignment with the extreme heat and constant noise made as steam passed through a small weight on top of the canner lid. The frequent slamming of the wooden screen door as the other children went in and out of the house reminded Mildred that she was a prisoner to the hot woodstove and the pressure canner.

I don't know that my mother ever had fun nor did she expect to have fun. Fun was certainly not her goal, but I do believe that she felt contentment, peace, and a sense of joy. She was a slow-moving person who managed to accomplish a lot because she worked steadily from early morning until ten o'clock at night. Because she was so calm and her movements were methodical, she did not appear to be tired or overworked—but I'm sure she was.

Walking with God in the Backwoods

A trait that my mother had which I admired greatly was her self-discipline. She always got up early and had a regular routine. Breakfast was served, dishes were washed, beds were made, and the floors were being swept by the time the sun was up.

A stack of firewood that had been carried into the living room each night during the winter months left particles of wood, dirt, and sawdust on the floor each morning. Ashes were shoveled from the wood-burning stove into a pan to be carried outside. That task always left a fog of ashes floating in the air and powdery ashes on the floor.

A pile of muddy shoes and wet boots were left at night to dry near the hot stove. In the morning, we carried our shoes or boots to the porch and beat them together to dislodge the clumps of dried mud from the tread. If it was too cold to go on the porch, we picked the clumps of dried mud off and put them in the ash pan. Even when we tried to be careful, lots of dirt was tracked inside the house.

Dust was a constant and discouraging battle for women who lived as we did. As the sun shined through the bare windows without curtains or shades, we observed the swirling dust motes being stirred up by Mama's broom. Leaving the dusty house behind, we headed off to the bus stop in the clean crisp air on a wintery morning. Smoke from the chimney waved a gentle good-bye and the scent of smoke from the wood burner called after us: "Y'all come back, ye hear?"

Mabel Margaret Motes Bufford

We could not avoid having to live somewhat primitive, but Mama would not allow us to be uncivilized. With regular sit-down meals, she maintained dignity in the way our family dined. At every meal, food was poured from the skillets, pots, and pans into breakable serving bowls. Considering that all water had to be hand-pumped and then heated on the wood-burning stove for "doin' dishes," she chose not to eliminate serving bowls to lessen the large amount of dishes to be washed. Before we were seated at the table, we took turns washing our hands and faces in a porcelain wash pan. Everyone used the same water and dried on the same terry cloth bath towel that hung from a nail. No one was allowed to fill their plate or take a bite until all were seated and my father had recited this table grace:

"Our most kind and gracious Heavenly Father, as we come before you, we thank you for the food that is set before us. We ask you to bless this food to the nourishment of our bodies and to feed our spirit with the pure and the undefiled. Sanctify our home and bless us and then go with us through the remainder of this day and we'll give you the praise and the glory in Jesus's name."

Daddy said that table grace three times a day for over fifty years. Acting as the priest of his home, he not only blessed the food, but he spoke a blessing over his family each day as well. I never asked my parents where the prayer came from. Mike told me that ritual began while we attended the Baptist church called Cooper and Hanes. I assumed Mama

Walking with God in the Backwoods

found it in church literature and suggested that Daddy could memorize it and recite it. It was an excellent prayer that covered everything.

It was Mama's intention to teach her girls to have a spirit of excellence. After each cleaning assignment, she included the admonition, "Don't just give it a lick and a promise." This meant that we were to do a thorough job, one we could be proud of. This applied mainly to my sisters and me because we were expected to do household cleaning while the boys helped with the chores outdoors.

All leftover food scraps were carried to the barn cats and the hound dogs or put into the slop bucket for the pigs. At the end of the day, Daddy would add water and a powdery substance called shorts to the slop bucket. He carried the five-gallon bucket of slop to the pen where the pigs were kept and poured it into their feeding trough. On one occasion, there were no biscuits left from the meal and no food scraps for the dogs to eat. I took note that my mother mixed biscuit dough and baked a fresh batch of biscuits especially for the hungry dogs. I knew she was not fond of the dogs, but she felt compassion for them and would not leave them to suffer.

If a drinking glass, plate, or bowl was broken, we carried it to a special rock in the yard and hammered it carefully. We did not quit until the glass particles were as grains of sand. Mama said the chickens would eat the particles of glass, and it would help them to digest their food. As far as she was concerned, every discarded thing could serve a new purpose.

When the boys' blue jeans were worn out, Mama could usually find some part of them worth saving to use for patches on another pair of denim jeans or overalls. All scraps of new fabric were saved for piecing a pretty quilt top. When the quilt tops were finished, they were taken to Grandma West's house, for she had space in her large bedroom for a quilting frame which hung from the ceiling. My mother and grandmother sewed many homemade quilts that were used as wedding gifts for loved ones. Fabric that was obviously old was kept in a ragbag to be used for bandages or cleaning rags. Disposable rags were nicer than using a handkerchief for blowing our nose at home for the pieces of rags could be deposited in the wood-burning stove rather than in the laundry.

Mama taught us to use a paring knife at a very young age and how to "go savin'" when we peeled large tubs of tomatoes or peaches for canning. She taught us to be careful, deliberate, and thrifty. There was an old New England saying that had been passed down from Grandma West's side of the family: Use it up, wear it out, make it do, or do without.

Slow songs were Mama's favorites, and many of them she had learned as a young woman while going to church at Hankins near Grubbs. Though she did not have a beautiful singing voice, she could carry a tune. Because there was so much silence at our house, we listened when she sang bits and pieces of songs. Mama did not sing as much in the fields as she did while doing housework; some of her favorite songs were "'Tis So Sweet to Trust in Jesus," "I'll Meet You in the Morning,"

"God Put a Rainbow in the Clouds," and "Wonderful Words of Life." She sang two very sad and haunting songs, "Throw Out the Lifeline" and "When They Ring Those Golden Bells for You and Me." During times that Mama was praying for rain, she would sing "Showers of Blessings." Andrew said his very first memory was that of sitting on Mama's lap while she sang her favorite song, "The Lily of the Valley." That's the song she requested for her funeral.

—∿—

Ministering to the Lord

Sometimes, Mama was desperately lonely in the backwoods where the Lord was her only friend. What Mama discovered about ministering to the Lord, she learned while struggling to survive emotional distress, depression and physical ailments.

Ministering to the Lord is beyond prayer and supplication for it is not about ourselves and not about others. It goes even further than giving thanks. It is saying to God the words that He most wants to hear—beautiful words of praise and adoration that come from the heart. When Mama didn't know beautiful words to say, she recited words that David the Psalmist had written. In the stillness and the solitude of the backwoods, Mama learned the art of ministering to the Lord as she memorized verses from the book of Psalms and quoted them to the Lord. As she communed with her Heavenly Father, His comforting scriptures gave her counsel and strength to keep going. Few people knew my mother well enough to be her friend, but I am sure that God delighted in her for she was a friend of God.

The Psalms were written under the inspiration of the Holy Spirit and give us insight into God's Love Language. Mama's favorite books of the Bible were Isaiah and Psalms, and her favorite chapter in the Bible was Psalms 145. Even as a child, I memorized the first four verses of that chapter as a result of hearing it frequently quoted.

The early years of a child's life may be more important for transferring Christian values than we have realized, for it is a time when parents have the greater influence and opportunity. A mother plays an important role in helping to form a child's character much like the role which the Holy Spirit plays in her own life. The gentle Holy Spirit whispers corrective words to all of us like a loving mother would say to her small child. While her child's character is being formed, it seems that a good mother reinforces the child's conscience. Could it be that a good mother acts as the conscience for her child until such a time as he has developed his own?

Blessed with Favor

I believe my mother found favor with the Lord. Though her circumstances did not outwardly change during those years in the backwoods, wheels were set in motion and the benefits that her children reap today may be a direct result of her prayers. God has promised to give his followers the desires of their heart. My mother's greatest desires were for her children, grandchildren, and future generations. She even prayed for the spouses of each one before they were born.

Before American mothers had the benefit of modern conveniences, they were often terribly limited by their circumstances. Many of the stay-at-home mothers lived through their children. It seemed that a mother enjoyed her sons' accomplishments and exploits as much or even more than the father did. Psalms 127:3 says, "Lo children are an heritage of the Lord and the fruit of the womb is his reward."

Often, when a woman in the Bible found favor with God, she was blessed in the area of motherhood—God gave her a son and blessed the son with favor. It was not characteristic of God to reward a woman by relieving her of the role of mothering her children. It appears that the Lord does not value or elevate other roles for women higher than He esteems mothering. In Malachi 2:15, we find that God's objective for marriage and family is, "That he might seek a godly seed." Though successful women achieve great and noble things that are admirable and beneficial, all of society suffers when women fail at mothering.

> One generation shall praise thy works to another, and shall declare thy mighty acts.
>
> —Psalms 145:4

When the Roll Is Called Up Yonder

DURING THE EARLY SUMMER, MAMA stayed at the house to cook dinner while Daddy was driving the tractor in a field far from home. She sent all five of her children to chop cotton in the vast seventeen-acre field near the house. While we were alone and expected to work, we tried to find ways to amuse ourselves so we could survive the monotony of such a long, boring day.

The sun quickly became hot and miserable and the humidity excessive. As we continued to work during the midmorning heat, we became sun parched and extremely thirsty. We designated the youngest child, Andrew, to be the water boy, and he went to the house to fetch a large glass jug of cool water. Passing the refreshing water around for the second time, we drank and drank. After our bellies were full of water, Andrew discovered there was a sloshing sound inside his belly when he moved about. It so amazed each of us that we began jumping up and down to hear the water sloshing inside our bellies as well. Soon, we felt deathly ill with a dreadful upset stomach. The extreme Arkansas heat was bad enough, but it was horrible to work in this physical condition. To the dismay of our mother, all her child laborers returned to the house to "lie around" while feeling ill. By afternoon, we had recovered and were sent back to the field.

Storm Clouds

While chopping cotton in the oppressive heat, my siblings and I welcomed the dark clouds that gathered over our heads and blocked the afternoon sun. We kept working, for it was cooler at that time than it would be the next day with the hot sun and high humidity. We stopped to assess the situation as distant thunder directed our attention to a second layer of approaching storm clouds. While standing idle, Andrew noticed the hair on top our heads was standing straight up like a severe case of static electricity. Each of us pointed at the other as we laughed about the unusual phenomenon. We were unaware that the hair-raising experience was an indication that the conditions were right for lightning to strike in our location at any moment. Suddenly, there was a deafening clap of thunder directly above our head; it was so loud that it put the fear of God in us. Each of us dropped our hoe to the ground right where we were standing and ran immediately to the house.

Many years later, we were informed that we had foolishly risked our life. In the same way, all are becoming aware of the possibility of Christ's imminent return to earth. Like watching storm clouds that move ever closer, we can see the signs of the end time. Will there be a big event like the clap of thunder to warn us that the end is upon us and the door of opportunity is closing? At what moment will stragglers know to drop whatever they are doing and rush into the ark of safety? We cannot know the exact day or hour that the Messiah will call his elect to meet him in the air, but we must not be oblivious to the warning signs.

Two of society's most important values are integrity and dignity. We can be sure the Lord will return before there is no honor among men, no purity among women, and no innocence among children.

—∞—

The Storm Cellar

With thunderstorms from spring through summer in Arkansas, tornadoes were a serious concern. Daddy often stood at the back screen door during a storm to watch the

Mabel Margaret Motes Bufford

ominous clouds and listen for a sound like that of a freight train in the distance. Without benefit of television or radio weather reports, Daddy was responsible to determine if our family was in the path of a tornado and if we should go to the storm cellar in the backyard. The cellar was a deep hole dug in the ground with the unused dirt making a steep mound around the outside of the hole. With a frame made of logs inside the large hole, it was like a dark dungeon with its roof at ground level. When he said to go, we ran through the rain to the cellar without covering our heads.

Daddy lifted a trapdoor on the side of the mound for us to enter and held a flashlight to light the way. With hearts beating fast, we all filed inside and sat down on a bench that Daddy had built for the dreary cellar. We looked on as he lit a kerosene lantern, which dangled from a hook in the ceiling. In the glow of the lantern, Daddy could see a black snake lying inside on the ledge where the wooden frame stopped and the roof began. He calmly pointed him out, and we all looked that direction. No one screamed or said a word. Since Daddy wasn't afraid, we weren't either. "He's trying to get out of the storm too," Daddy said with a gentle tone of understanding. The snake didn't move, except for his tongue, while we sat shivering in the cool cellar with water dripping from our hair. You can be sure each of us kept an eye on the snake.

"I dreamed this last night," Audrey said in a matter-of-fact tone. I turned my gaze to look intently at her face, hoping to see some hint of emotion and to hear more about it. She showed no emotion and said no more. Our family sat patiently as we listened to the rain beating rhythmically on the roof of the cellar. Several times after the summer of 1960, Audrey had prophetic dreams, and she would make the same comment. She probably would have told me every detail if I had probed, but I didn't feel that I should.

Hired Hands

When we had hired hands to help with chopping our cotton, they were to be in the field at 6:00 a.m. Daddy had to be there early to file every hoe and to "line 'em out" or give instructions. The grass was usually wet with dew that time in the morning, and our shoes would be soggy for the first few hours. That's why my siblings and I preferred to chop cotton without shoes. Daddy provided a jug of water for all the hired hands to drink which was left setting in the truck that was parked under a shade tree. We didn't have a fancy insulated jug with "ice water," but instead, we had a gallon-size glass jug with a burlap bag stitched around it to keep the water cool for a while. There was no ice in the water since we had no refrigerator and no electricity. Everyone drank from the same jug and appreciated the water.

We had an hour to eat dinner and rest before we had to be back in the field at 1:00 p.m. and chop cotton until "quittin' time" at 6:00 p.m. Since we worked for our dad, my siblings and I did not always get paid. Daddy wasn't as likely to pay us at cotton chopping time in the spring as he was in the fall at cotton picking time. The money which he had borrowed to "make a crop" had to be spent very carefully so it would last until harvest time. Audrey and I were small and frail and could not hold up well to work hard all day like an adult. We always tried harder if "hired hands" were in the field with us.

By this time, there was enough prosperity that people in our community preferred not to hire out to work in the cotton fields anymore. Daddy hired our cousins Olivee and Thelma to spend a week to help us finish chopping the cotton. They sure helped to make the job a lot more pleasant for Audrey and me. Sixteen-year-old Olivee and fourteen-year-old Audrey were interested in boys and were looking forward to dating. Thelma and I were entertained by listening to the bigger girls' conversation. My younger siblings, Joe, Mildred, and Andrew, stayed at the house with Mama during the morning while she did the cooking and housework. Because Joe was ten years old, Mildred was eight, and Andrew was seven, they would only be required to work half a day in the field. After Mama's housework was done, the noon meal was served, and dishes were washed, she took the three younger children to the field in the afternoon and had them to work alongside her.

When the cotton was "laid by," in July, Audrey and I went away to the Ozark Mountains with Olivee and Thelma to spend a week with Uncle Jesse's oldest daughter, Ella Mae, who had young girls near our age. Another one of Uncle Jesse's daughters, Hazel, had planned to preach a short revival at a church there in a community called Five Mile, near Drasco. We were eager to go to the revival each night and lend our support. As usual, local kids and teenagers were motivated to attend and to invite their neighbors when they heard that several other teenagers would be there from out of town.

Visiting Mike's Apartment

Mike drove our family to Memphis for a visit to his apartment for the first time and to visit the zoo again. We were eager to see how Mike lived in the big city where his way of life was new to us.

In preparation for dinner, we went to a supermarket where Mike bought several pot pies. Audrey helped Mike in the kitchen where she enjoyed getting to bake the pot pies in a modern oven. It was quite a change from the wood-burning stove at home. We had never eaten pot pies before, and we all agreed that they tasted really good.

Mike was eager for each of his siblings to take a shower, for we had never experienced a shower before. To keep Mildred from being afraid of the water, I agreed to take a shower with her, but my presence proved to be of little value. When the warm water pelted her in the face, it took her breath away. She disliked it and chose rather to stand with her head outside the shower stall with the plastic shower curtain tucked under her

Mabel Margaret Motes Bufford

chin. When it was Joe's and Andrew's turn, they chose to shower together. After they were finished, Mike asked what they thought of it. Joe exclaimed, "I almost drowned!" No one had explained to the young boys how to turn the water on and that both hot and cold water was available in a modern shower. They happened to turn only the cold water on and endured an icy-cold shower. We were thankful they had not turned on only the hot water and been severely injured.

Mike told us his memories of coming to Memphis for the first time. He said he knew no one in the big city who could "show him the ropes." A college counselor had advised him to get a room at the YMCA and begin the search for employment before college classes began.

Being a teenager of nineteen and having no car or driver's license, Mike arrived by Greyhound bus. Though he could walk short distances, traveling about town on the city buses took much of his savings. Knowing that he could not call home and get more money, he carefully rationed every cent. He did not know that a person must work two weeks before receiving the first paycheck. A week or so after starting his first job, the money began to run out.

Mike had not yet cultivated a friendship which would permit him to confide in another that he was broke and hungry. Feeling socially awkward, he chose to suffer in silence. Mike worked for a few days without food and fasted until the paycheck came.

The trip to Memphis was an exciting adventure, and we appreciated Mike for being such a good big brother. Often, I felt bad for Mike because he did not have a big brother when he needed one. Then, I remembered that "there is a friend that sticks closer than a brother" (Prov. 18:24).

Though it was hard for Mike to imagine any good coming from the painful experience, Jesus stated that the Father in heaven would reward believers openly for fasting (see Matt. 6:18).It took Mike seven years to achieve his bachelor of science degree in chemistry as he worked his way through college. During his career as a chemist, Mike had several patents for products that were put into commercial use.

Dynamite

Our family undertook a big project during the fall of 1961—we built a road. Well, what we created was a *roadway*. Daddy cut down all the trees in a straight line from the front yard to the county road, which is called Flag Slough Lane. When there was nothing left standing but stumps, he went to the store and bought dynamite, blasting caps and a roll of dynamite fuse.

While we were working toward building the road, Grandma West, in her eighties, fell at her home and broke her hip. Mama had to stay with her at the hospital in Jonesboro. Audrey and I were assigned to take over the cooking, dishwashing, and housework. I'm sure Mama was greatly distressed by having to leave her husband to care for five children while he had a big project requiring dynamite. I suspect she did a lot of praying while sitting with Grandma hour after hour.

Daddy made a handy tool for digging deep holes underneath a stump so he could place dynamite in it to blow the stump out of the ground. He attached a four-inch auger bit on the end of a pipe that was about four feet long. At the other end of the pipe, there was a loop secured onto the pipe with screws where a wooden handle could be inserted. All my siblings and I took turns twisting the auger as we dug holes at an angle underneath the stumps. We stopped digging when Daddy was satisfied that we had reached the point where the center of the stump should be.

Being a smart man, Daddy made sure that the blasting caps were stored separate from the dynamite and everything was handled carefully. He made a hole in the end of a blasting cap and inserted a length of special dynamite fuse and clamped it tight with his wire pliers. He made a hole in the end of a stick of dynamite with his pocket knife and inserted the blasting cap with the fuse dangling. He squeezed the dynamite tightly shut around the cap and taped two other sticks of dynamite to it. The bundle of dynamite was inserted into the hole under the stump as far as Daddy could reach and a stick was used to push it in farther if needed. Daddy had my siblings and me to stand about a hundred yards away before he struck a match to the fuse; then he ran and stood with us as everyone held their

Walking with God in the Backwoods

ears to shield from the deafening explosion. It was a thrill to watch the stump fly twenty feet in the air amid a shower of roots, dirt, and debris. Being less than a mile away, the neighbors probably found the explosions unnerving as they endured this chapter in our lives.

We went cautiously to see the gaping hole that had been left in the ground and braved the fumes and the fog which made everyone feel a little lightheaded. At the end of the day, the stumps were loaded onto a sled Daddy had built to pull behind the tractor. Brush piles scattered about smoldered continuously with the daily supply of stumps. The younger children, Joe, who had just turned eleven, Mildred who was almost nine, and Andrew at seven years old, thoroughly enjoyed their new job. Each child carried something or played a role that was vital to the process. Our farm became a kid's paradise having both open fires and explosives. The only reason Daddy could risk letting the children help was because they were capable of being perfectly obedient to instructions.

Working with dynamite affected my father and made his blood veins become noticeably larger. It caused his blood pressure to go up and his heart to beat a little harder. As the job progressed, Daddy had a few bouts of bleeding from the nose and had to take a break from the work to rest a while.

When the stumps had been successfully removed, the Poinsett County road commissioner was contacted, and a road grader was dispatched to form a ditch and level a road. Since the county completed the road, they got to name it. They chose to call it *Gap Road*. I would have preferred a prettier name; something like *Linger Lane* would have been nice.

The Old Red Rooster

My siblings and I were home alone one day when Daddy went to bring our mother home from sitting with Grandma at the hospital. Audrey and I thought we would impress our parents by having a meal of fried chicken on the table when they returned. This required that we kill a rooster, pick the feathers off, and butcher it. We had seen it done before and had even helped Mama a little with the process. It seemed simple enough, and we were sure we could do it without any adult supervision.

First, I singled out one rooster and chased him for several minutes only to have my attention diverted to a different rooster. Audrey and I must have chased the roosters for a half an hour. Before we were totally exhausted, I caught the biggest one. I carried the heavy rooster with both its legs together in my two hands and its head almost dragging on the ground. The rooster looked fierce and even larger with its feathers ruffled and its wings spread out as if he was preparing to take flight. I managed to get the heavy rooster lifted up onto the chop block with its head in the right position. Audrey lifted the axe high above her head and was prepared to take the rooster's head off with one swift blow. I began having second

Walking with God in the Backwoods

thoughts about it, but it was too late to tell Audrey. So I jerked the chicken back just as the axe fell. But I didn't quite get it off the chop block in time. Seeing that the rooster's beak and a portion of his face had been chopped off, I was aghast and let go of his legs. We watched in horror as the stunned rooster walked around for a few seconds before going under the house to seek shelter and safety.

When our weary parents returned from their long day at the hospital, we told them the story of our good intentions and the dreadful outcome. Daddy fussed at us because we had not even considered doing the barnyard chores so they would not have that to do upon their return. He said the rooster had to be killed because it would not be able to eat and would die slowly of starvation. Mama was extremely annoyed with us for causing them extra work. Daddy got his rifle and told us to stand behind him while he lay on the ground to take aim at the rooster as it walked about under the house.

Daddy had to crawl under the house to drag the dead rooster out. A fire had been built in the cook stove so Mama could boil water to douse the rooster in to make his feathers easier to pick out by hand. The wet feathers smelled awful. When the rooster appeared naked, Daddy had to hold it over some burning papers to singe the down-type feathers off. The burning feathers smelled just as bad or even worse than the wet feathers. The intestines had to be removed, and the chicken had to be washed carefully and cut into serving-size pieces for cooking. By the time the meal was ready, I was thoroughly sickened by the process and could not eat any of the meat. I have never tried to kill another chicken, and I always buy the meat precut so I will not be reminded of the ole red rooster.

—m—

Mike Finds a Wife

Mike was blessed to find Erlene, a young woman in Memphis who was perfectly suited to be his wife. On the day before their wedding, Mike drove three hours from Memphis to our house in Arkansas and spent the night. Around daylight the next morning on August 25, 1962, Mike drove Mama, Audrey, Mildred, and me to Memphis to attend the wedding. We arrived in the big city early and went shopping. As we strolled leisurely down the sidewalk along the store fronts, we ate from a large bag of popcorn that Mike had purchased for us to share. He bought a new dress for Audrey, Mildred, and for me at a store called *The Three Sisters*. We thought the name of the store was a very appropriate place for Mike to take his three sisters, but we would not forget to think of Kathy—the fourth sister.

Mike seemed perfectly calm and relaxed and got us to the church in plenty of time for the afternoon wedding. The bride was beautiful and so were the bridesmaids. Being a talented seamstress, Erlene had sewn her own lacy wedding gown. The only way in which Mike's nervousness was evident to his bride was in the fact that his hands felt icy cold to her touch

Walking with God in the Backwoods

as he slipped the ring on her finger. I thought the wedding ceremony was very nice but surprisingly short compared to our church services at Harmony Grove.

After having cake and punch at the home of Erlene's parents, the bridesmaids decorated Mike's car with a Just Married sign. They took great delight in attaching tin cans to dangle noisily from the bumper. Mike and Erlene had plans to drive us back home and leave from our house to honeymoon in Hardy, Arkansas. We must have looked a sight as we pulled away from the curb with cans rattling and the decorated car loaded down with Mike's family members. Both he and Erlene were a good sport about it and acted as it was perfectly normal. As soon as we turned the corner, Mike stopped the car and took all the decorations off. Mama was blessed that her new daughter-in-law would become a best friend to her and a cherished member of our family. Right away, Erlene began saving her newspapers and magazines to bring to our house when she came for visits. Audrey enjoyed the magazines; my mother enjoyed hours of pleasure in reading the newspapers. Mike and Erlene have celebrated fifty-three years together.

—∿∿—

A Bountiful Harvest, 1962

As a child, I was only vaguely aware of the good life presented on television, for we lived without benefit of modern conveniences and electricity until I was thirteen years old. We made a good crop in 1962, the best we had ever made. Finally, we had enough prosperity to have electricity wired into the farmhouse on Mildred's tenth birthday. We baked a cake, and Daddy bought soda pop to celebrate the occasion. We didn't often celebrate a birthday with more than a home-baked cake, even soda pop was a rare treat to us.

Daddy surprised Mama by hauling home a used couch and chair to match. The cheap furniture was covered with vinyl rather than fabric. We were just happy to have a couch and padded chair because we'd never had one before. Straight-backed, cane-bottom chairs were all we had to sit on in the living room. On the same truck load was a used kitchen table with chrome legs and a Formica top with padded chairs that were covered by matching vinyl. We were eager to dismantle the old wooden table and bench in the kitchen that Daddy had made of rough lumber. The homemade table had served us well for many years with a colorful print "oil cloth" to cover the surface. We were "coming on up" in the world.

—∿—

Getting a Television, 1963

Audrey invited Jean Blanchard, her best girl friend from Weiner High School, to spend the weekend. Mama was surprised to find Audrey in the house reading a novel while her guest had been left to entertain herself. Jean sat alone in the yard for hours happily cracking hickory nuts and eating the small amount of meat she got from each one. Audrey and Jean had a comfortable relationship that allowed them to just be themselves without fear of being misunderstood.

Audrey and Mama shared a great love for reading. The *Saturday Evening Post* magazine that Aunt Mabel gave to Mike as a gift subscription was our family's single window to the modern world for many years. Audrey checked out books from the school library so Mama could sit and read them to the family during the winter months when it got dark early and we were indoors more. Those reading sessions would soon be left by the wayside.

We needed a television badly, for we often felt left out of conversations at school that referred to television shows the students had viewed the night before. We heard discussions about the Ed Sullivan show almost every Monday at school, yet we never saw it. I heard kids laughing about the crazy hillbillies and the activities of Granny and the Clampett family; I cringed inside because we were living in the same outdated fashion that the Clampetts had left behind. If they were considered crazy, then what would people think of us if they ever were to "find out."

Television viewing had created another language which everyone seemed to speak except the kids in our family. I admired the students that could recite a list of shows that came on each night of the week and tell which channel they came on and their time slot. We heard students talk about ordering pizza, and we did not even know what pizza was. If only we had a television, we might become familiar with the things other students talked about. Audrey did find a recipe in a magazine for pizza pie and made some for us in aluminum pie pans. Daddy invited Uncle Jesse's family over to eat with us. They had never tasted pizza either. Audrey was good at cooking and baking deserts and was a great asset in the kitchen.

In the spring of 1963, after I turned fourteen, we got a new black-and-white television. There was a girl in my class named Sue, and she was like a walking TV guide. I told her we would have our first television when we got home from school that day and asked what shows she would recommend. While giving me the lineup, she mentioned *The Flintstones*, and I made a mental note of that specific title, its channel, and its time slot. I was so disappointed when I discovered that it was not a good Western as I had hoped it would be.

My siblings and I were totally unprepared for the emotional upheaval we would experience as a result of watching television. Many things that were suspenseful to others caused us to feel distraught. It was not unusual that my sisters and I would have to slip out of the living room because we could not bear to watch scenes depicting sadness or trauma. We could not handle seeing gunfights and people in mortal danger. Mildred had to go outside the house when the Lone Ranger started shooting. We often left the room to cry in the privacy of our bedrooms when we were deeply touched by the suffering or sadness of television characters. Though it was necessary that we get a television and observe a portion of the modern world, we could not make ourselves just like other people. Not because we were any better than others but because we were destined to be different; getting a television did not change that fact.

> The Lord taketh pleasure in them that fear him,
> in those that hope in his mercy.

—Psalms 147:11

14

I'll Fly Away

THE STUDENTS AT THE WEINER school were kind and made no comments about me being poor. Any discrimination I experienced could be attributed to my own perception and sensitivity. If each student had been experiencing poverty at the same time, as happened during the Depression era, the stigma and shame could have been alleviated. Rarely did I visit a person in my peer group that had less than my family. However, I did visit in the home of one articulate young girl who had a dirt floor in the kitchen. Though my house had wooden floors throughout, I took comfort in the knowledge that I was not alone in deprivation. I felt a degree of relief in knowing that poverty had other victims as well.

My memories of farm life in Arkansas include that of picking cotton along with hardworking women who suffered in poverty. One mother, Minie Duty, was nine months pregnant and left the field—in labor—to give birth to her sixth child. As a sensitive teenager, I was stricken with the indignity of the poor woman's plight. Minie captured my attention because she was a tough lady who worked like a man and often drove a tractor in the fields. She was one of the first young women to break with the traditional role for Southern women in cotton farming country. Many of the older farm wives had no driver's license, for they had not learned how to drive an automobile.

Sex Ed

My mother did not tell the girls in our family about the facts of life. My older sister informed me, and it was our bold cousin, Olivee, that enlightened her. Farm children do have an advantage over children of other means, for they can observe the cycle of reproduction among the farm animals from mating to birth. Partly from that observation, I had an understanding of the fact that sex makes babies.

Sex education was not the norm in schools when I attended. The most necessary information concerning puberty was given during the sixth grade to the boys and girls in a separate group. A reel-to-reel film was shown by a projector on a pull-up screen giving us beneficial knowledge of human anatomy. We were all embarrassed.

As a lazy person, I was not abounding in the virtue of self-discipline and self-control, but I did have a desire to please God and to please my family. I cared about the consequences of my actions on the ones I loved most. I cared what people would think, not only about me but about my family. There was an unspoken obligation of each family member to protect the dignity of their family's name. Also, I had a healthy fear of God that was instilled in me from sermons at church and from my parents at home with scriptures that warn: "Be sure your sins will find you out" (Num. 32:23) and "Be not deceived: God is not mocked: for whatsoever a man soweth, that shall he also reap" (Gal. 6:7). Those verses led me to believe that my sin would put me at odds with God, and I dared not to take the risk. In my case, scripture verses proved to be an excellent prevention for promiscuity and unwanted pregnancy. My having praying parents was of great benefit also, for the path of purity is often paved with the parents' prayers.

Though we experienced great family loyalty, my sisters and I depended on each other for understanding and consoling. My parents seemed more like grandparents to me, for they had married in their mid-thirties and looked old when compared to the parents of my classmates. My sister, Audrey, less than two years older than I, played the role of confidant and substitute mother. In reality, farm life required that my parents work such long hours that we were often overlooked.

It took an injury, illness, or an injustice to elicit tender moments from my parents, yet we had adequate care in the area of physical needs.

—⁓—

Singing Specials

Audrey and I sang special songs at our church and often sang when we went to district rallies where we represented our church. Our youth were called CAs, which stood for Christ Ambassadors. It was a special blessing from God that we were privileged to grow up in church. The youth rallies were an exciting outing for us since we rarely went anywhere, except church and school. Our family, our church, and God were our life.

While Uncle Jesse's family lived close to Uno, they attended church with us at Harmony Grove for a year or more. We thoroughly enjoyed having relatives living nearby. Our cousins Olivee and Thelma teamed up with Audrey and me, and we sang together in church and at rallies. We sang one time at a revival at Long Creek Baptist, the place where our grandparents David and Mary had once attended church. Uncle Jesse had been the song leader there at one time when he was a younger man. Olivee suggested that we should walk next door to the church and buy lemons at Bud and Letha Wright's store to eat before the service. She had read that some professional singers eat lemons before a performance to clear their throat so they can sing more clearly. (We were taking our singing serious.)

Walking with God in the Backwoods

A group of four teenage girls, each having hair down to the waist, was the Motes girls' trademark. Olivee and Thelma had dark hair while Audrey and I had blond hair. Our grandparents, David and Mary, would have been pleased with our little singing group.

Our church congregation sang hymns from the hymnal, but the special songs were often the modern songs sung by famous people on the radio. Olivee and Thelma taught us country Gospel songs that they had learned from the radio and from the various churches where they had attended. Around that time, we became aware of a song called "A House of Gold," and it soon became Audrey's favorite. She wanted me to sing it with her as a special at church, but I didn't want to because it had a high note that caused me to strain too much, but we sang it around the house. Hank Williams wrote and recorded the song.

> "A House of Gold"
> People steal, they cheat and lie
> For wealth and what it will buy
> Don't they know on the judgment day
> Gold and silver will melt away
>
> I'd rather be in a deep, dark grave
> And know that my poor soul was saved
> Than to live in this world in a house of gold
> And deny my God and lose my soul

What good is gold and silver, too
If your heart's not good and true
Sinner hear me when I say
Fall down upon your knees and pray

I'd rather be in a deep, dark grave
And know that my poor soul was saved
Than to live in this world in a house of gold
And deny my God and lose my soul
And deny my God and lose my soul.

The Boyfriend

During the year that Audrey turned sixteen, Mama and Daddy were aware that she would soon want to date. They were concerned because there were few honorable young men available. Daddy saw a teen boy driving a tractor in a field near our farm, and he introduced himself and took note of the boy's name. Being a good worker was one of the greater qualities that Daddy looked for in his estimation of any man. Daddy and Mama discussed the young man, and Mama asked Audrey if she knew the boy from school and what she thought of him.

Audrey was annoyed at their attempt to shop for a suitable boyfriend for her. She had thought about her future and what she wanted in a man and what she did not want. She told Mama, "I don't want a tractor driver, and I don't want a hillbilly." (That was exactly what my father was). I personally did not see anything wrong with either of those two choices and didn't see any need for her to further limit the possibilities.

Audrey was a person of few words, and she could command respect for herself. While being a little mother to her brothers and sisters, she had become quite the disciplinarian. She shared some character traits with our dad—one being her ability to take swift action when something displeased her. Audrey could verbally set her siblings straight, and we respected her. For that reason, Daddy sometimes called her Spitfire.

Living with her family in the backwoods, Audrey feared she had little chance of meeting her prince charming. She prayed about her situation, and I'm sure Mama and Daddy did too. Like pawns being moved on a chess board, God brought her prince charming to her.

Aubrey Dean Huskey had recently moved from the area of Marked Tree to Tuckerman, Arkansas. Tuckerman was less than twenty miles from where our house was in the backwoods. But that was still a long way. How the two of them found each other was amazing to me. Aubrey Dean's new friend, Bobby, was eager to introduce him to some girls. Bobby had heard of the Motes girls, and he wanted to take Aubrey Dean to find them. The person who told Bobby of the girls was most likely thinking of the Jesse Motes family who had lived in the area of Denton Island. But our relatives had moved to Uno, and the young men were unable to locate them. As they went farther into the country, they were given directions to our house.

From the living room window, Audrey saw an unfamiliar car pulling into our driveway on a boring Saturday afternoon on February 1, 1964. It was not unusual for hunters to talk to my father before they hunted in the woods near the property where we lived. Daddy stopped splitting stove wood and walked over to the car, eager to greet the visitors. The young men informed him that they were looking for the Motes family. My father introduced himself, and the young men found him to be approachable and pleasant.

As Aubrey Dean and Bobby stepped out of the car, Levi immediately engaged them in lively conversation which put them at ease. When Audrey saw that the visitors were not hunters or farm laborers, she suspected they were not there on business with Daddy. When Audrey walked outside to see who our visitors were, the young men were surprised to see a stunning slender girl with beautiful, long blond hair. It was Audrey's habit to wear simple cotton dresses at all times. Though she did not own makeup or jewelry, she didn't need it. Audrey easily maintained a dressed-up appearance even when she wasn't prepared to be seen.

—⟫—

Audrey's First Date

While Bobby had Levi's attention diverted, Aubrey Dean watched for his chance to wink at Audrey. When she responded with a shy smile, he knew this wonderful girl was receptive, and he could risk asking her dad if he could take her out. Audrey knew she could not go with the two strangers alone. She had to think quickly of an acceptable solution for the problem. She suggested that Dianne, a girlfriend from school, might be allowed to go out with them and be Bobby's blind date on short notice.

Audrey turned to Daddy and asked, "If Margaret goes with us, can we go to Dianne's house and ask if she can go out, and then we'll bring Margaret back?" It was a good plan.

"I reckon that would be all right," Daddy said. "Just be home at ten o'clock." Audrey rushed into the house to tell me the plan. Of course I was willing to do it just for her. I was not interested in the guys or in dating at all. This was my fifteenth birthday, and I had planned to watch my favorite shows on television. My parents and siblings would humor me on this occasion and let me decide what we would all watch together. (Having control of the television was a big deal in a large family.)

When we arrived at Dianne's house, she and her family were not at home. We waited around for a few minutes in case they might return; when they did not, Aubrey Dean drove us around for a while. When I saw that my plans were not going to work out, I began to fuss about what I was missing on television. I had waited all week to see those particular programs. I really should have been more agreeable and let Audrey enjoy her first date. Since I was being so childish, Audrey decided that they should take me home, and then they would drive Bobby to his house. That would allow her some time to be alone with Aubrey Dean.

They let me out of the car in the darkness, and I walked into the living room where my parents were sitting. I knew that they would be extremely upset with Audrey for going alone with the two strangers. Daddy asked, "Is Dianne with them?"

"Yeah," I lied. I kept walking so I would not be available for more conversation. That decision caused me to miss the television shows that I had so looked forward to. I felt so awful for blatantly lying to my parents. I felt awful because they believed me; they trusted me. I was extremely sorrowful and disappointed in myself. I was the only one who knew of the precarious situation Audrey had placed herself in, and I was the one who had caused the situation to evolve. With guilt crashing down upon me, I wished I had just stayed with her. At that moment, I felt an enormous weight of responsibility for her, and I was afraid.

Acting as an intercessor, I took spiritual responsibility. Like a mother prays for her child, I prayed for Audrey's safe return. I was too young to know much about intercession. Much later, I learned that an intercessor is a person who carries another to the throne of God on wings of prayer. At that moment, I was carrying my sister. It was the first time that I had thoughts like a mature person. That night was when I began to grow up.

Walking with God in the Backwoods

Many years later, I realized that the prophetic dream concerning my little sister's death was not just about her. In that dream, I was carrying Kathy and taking responsibility to protect her from the enemy of her soul. God was telling me that my role was that of an intercessor. It was strangely out of character for me to take charge, make a quick decision, work hard and fast, and accomplish a goal. Audrey had always been the capable leader, and our roles had suddenly been reversed. In the dream, I was taking charge like a big sister while Audrey was the follower.

Life-Altering Decisions

Audrey had fallen in love with the young man named Aubrey Dean Huskey. His name was amazingly similar to hers—Audrey Della. She reasoned aloud, "What are the chances of a guy and a girl having twin names for both first name and middle name. Also, what are the chances that they would be in the same age category and the same area of the state and to meet each other and both fall in love with the other? And if they were married, they would have the same initials." She was sure these unusual occurrences were a sign from God that Aubrey Dean was the right mate for her.

A typical date for Audrey and Aubrey Dean consist of driving around on a Saturday night. Aubrey Dean would come early for church on Sunday morning and would spend the afternoon with Audrey and go back to church with us on a Sunday night. On Sunday afternoon, they would drive around and go visiting. Often, they would let me and one of our girl friends from church go too. Aubrey Dean was the only young single man at the church at that time, and he seemed to feel out of place. We got to church early one Sunday evening and sat around and talked to others who had also arrived early. Cleveland and Katie Keller talked to Aubrey Dean about his need for salvation, and he knelt at the altar while they gathered around to pray with him.

Though she was only sixteen years old, Audrey did not choose to go back to school in the fall. It was not like her to quit anything, but she had a sense of urgency and was eager to get on with her life. Mama and Daddy knew the fire of sexual temptation for teens and young adults would be near impossible to quench, so they gave their consent quickly and easily for the two to be married. They had done their part of teaching morals, and they had trusted the Lord to bring the right person; their job was done, and they were at peace with the decision.

—⁓—

Audrey's Wedding

We had a visiting minister and his wife who came to Harmony Grove to promote youth clubs, Royal Rangers and Missionnets, for the children of the church. They were a young

Walking with God in the Backwoods

couple from the rural area near Tuckerman. Audrey made arrangements with them to perform the wedding ceremony after she and Aubrey Dean had dated for six months. The date was set for Monday morning July 27, 1964. Aubrey Dean came to get Audrey early that morning, and they drove to the minister's house. Audrey wore a blue dress she had made in the home economics class at Weiner High School. The fabric was a rayon blend which had embossed flowers.

As Audrey and Aubrey Dean approached the minister's house, they saw an extra automobile in the driveway and assumed the minister had unexpected company. Audrey and Aubrey drove passed and waited a distance down the road for the visitors to leave. After a while, they drove passed again only to find the car was still there. They waited again. When they could wait no longer, they returned to the minister's house and went to the door in spite of the visitors. Once inside, it was explained that the visiting couple had been invited to the wedding to serve as witnesses. Audrey and Aubrey Dean did not know witnesses were needed. The minister and his wife had seen them driving back and forth in front of the house and thought they were getting "cold feet" and might not go through with the ceremony.

Very little money was spent on the wedding ceremony, and there was no reception and no honeymoon. Money was more needed for the business of maintaining the home and sustaining an adequate standard of living. "The marriage was far more important than the wedding ceremony," Audrey reasoned. There had not even been a wedding shower, and the young couple had very little to "set up housekeeping." After the ceremony, Aubrey Dean took Audrey to his mother's house. He needed to get back to work for he had only taken off half a day from his job. His mother Annie Huskey went with them to the little house they had rented and spent the afternoon with Audrey so she would not be alone while the groom worked. She and Audrey became very close friends. Audrey loved the Huskey family, and they loved her. Aubrey Dean's mother, Annie Huskey, still lives alone at ninety-nine years old in 2015.

1965

Many Christian girls married husbands who had no interest in things of a spiritual nature and did not wish to attend church with them. It was not unusual to see a young man attend church while shopping for a good wife and then drop out after he had secured her hand in marriage. There was sadness that plagued those young women as they struggled to walk alone and to stay in church. Often, they became battle weary and gave up the fight. Is it possible that men will do whatever they have to do to get the wife they desire? Could it be that women have a civilizing effect on men and those men will only be as good as women require them be? It may be that women, especially mothers, are unaware of the power they possess, for if they were aware of it, they would surely use it—for Christ's sake.

At the ripe old age of sixteen, I was beginning to have fears that I might not find someone to love and might not have anyone who would choose to love me. There were no boys attending my church except for my little brothers, Joe and Andrew, and boys in their age group. Church attendance was not considered manly by the young men in the 1960s. I was vaguely aware that a celebrity named James Dean had greatly influenced the teenage boys as their bad-boy masculine role model. Young men began to emulate Elvis Presley and other rock and roll stars with their choice of hairstyles and demeanor. I prayed about my concern and said to my Heavenly Father, "If you don't send me a Christian boy, I will never date"; at that moment, I meant it.

I imagined the possibility that I might never be married and would have to deal with my future as an old maid. But God knew my deepest desires. He knew that I would like to have a husband and a family. Plan B was the possibility that I might have to provide for myself as a single lady, I began to consider what might make a suitable career. My thoughts turned to the possibility of becoming a nurse, but God knew I was not well suited for that kind of work. I did not want to remain poor and struggling, but I did not know how to change my circumstances. I just knew that I did not want to stay on the farm and work in the cotton fields. I wanted prosperity and nice things, but I'd have to leave the farm to find it. I determined to watch for an opportunity to present itself for a better way of life.

Hope for My Future

On a Sunday morning during the summer of 1965, we had arrived at the church long before starting time. It was my father's responsibility to unlock the church doors of our country church. It gave the children of the early arrivals a great opportunity to enjoy their friends before the services began. My girl friends and I were standing inside the building and looking out the window of a classroom when an unfamiliar car pulled into the parking area underneath the trees. It was a station wagon and it was full of people. Our church had few people and seldom had visitors. All the doors opened on the station wagon, and everyone began to pile out. There were boys—big boys—and lots of them. All the teenage girls gathered at the window and excitedly began to point toward a guy and say, "That's the one I want." There were more girls looking out the window than boys walking toward the church, so it happened that the one I had chosen was also wanted by my friend Deloris. "I know him," Deloris said as she pointed to the guy I wanted. "I chopped cotton with him. His name is Sammy Bufford."

I looked forward to being in the teen class with the visitors, but the teacher for the primary class was absent, and I was asked to be a substitute teacher for that class. My heart sank, but I tried not to let the disappointment show. I didn't like the fact that other young girls would be in the teen class with the new guys while I was separated from the group.

I taught the little children their lesson and dismissed them early. After returning the little children to their parents in the adult class, I rushed to the teen class. With their lesson finished as well, I was pleased to be included in the idle chatter. It was a perfect opportunity to hear answers to the usual questions about where the new teenagers were from and who they knew in the area. I was pleased to discover that Sam was eighteen and had recently graduated from Grubbs High School. During the worship portion of the service, the young men sat toward the back of the church, and I sat near the front. As I looked back at the boys sitting side by side on the pew, there was a discussion going on inside my head.

"Are you sure that is the one you want?"

"Yes, that's the one I want," I answered.

As soon as church was over, I went to Sam's sister, Angie, and questioned her about Sam. "Does he have a girlfriend?" I asked eagerly.

"Yeah," Angie answered. "He's dating someone right now." My heart sank again, and I determined to put him out of my mind. Sam and his family continued to come to church, and Sam even brought his girlfriend a few times before they drifted apart. Angie was near my age, and we became good friends. As collaborator, she was beneficial in letting Sam know that I was interested in a relationship with him. By

Mabel Margaret Motes Bufford

October, Sam and I were dating. The Lord had prepared a Christian for me to date, and I was only sixteen. Our dates would consist mostly of sitting together during church, and Sam driving me home afterward. Most often, there were several little brothers and sisters in the car with us.

I told Sam about the silly competition among the girls on the first day his family had attended our church. I confided to Sam, "Since Deloris said she knew you and had chopped cotton with you, I thought that you would choose to date her."

"Nah," he said with astonishment, "I chopped cotton with her all right. She picked up dirt clods and threw 'em at me. One hit me in the head and almost knocked me out."

At the time Sam and I met, he was working for a farmer, Lannas Ragsdale, at Pitts and had been driving a tractor. I was amused when I discovered that Sam was born at Drasco near Heber Springs which is in the mountains. The young man I had chosen was both a tractor driver and a hillbilly, just as my dad had been, but I didn't mind. I had asked God for a Christian young man, and what I had asked for—God had granted.

—∞—

Audrey, 1965

After they became married, Audrey and Aubrey Dean gradually drifted away from consistent church attendance at Harmony Grove. It was quite a distance to drive from their home in Tuckerman, and they had other family members

Walking with God in the Backwoods

that they should spend time with as well. We still saw them at least every two weeks since they both liked being socially involved. During one of Audrey's visits, she told me that Aubrey Dean had taken her swimming in a river. She had never been swimming before and was afraid of the water. The closest we had come to swimming when we were on the farm was to crawl around and splash in the road ditch after a big rain. There were so many water moccasins in our area that it was not a good idea to swim anywhere near Flag Slough.

Audrey said that she stepped into a drop-off in the river and fell under the deep water. With the muddy water over her head, she did not know which way was *up*. She struggled frantically for a few seconds before she felt Aubrey's grip on her arm. By then, she was terrified and began grabbing onto him as tightly as she could. She was still under the water and knew she could not live much longer without air. She knew she was going to die by drowning within the next minute. She told me that in her mind she saw printed words that looked like bold headlines in a newspaper which said "Woman drowns husband." When she read the words, she realized her husband was going to die too, and she would be the cause of his death. Because she loved him so much, she turned loose of him immediately so he could live. When Aubrey Dean was free of Audrey's grip, he was able to shove her back into the more shallow area where she could stand up. I have heard of a prophecy preacher that said the Lord gave him warnings of things to come by showing him newspaper

Mabel Margaret Motes Bufford

headlines that read as if it was reported after the event. I might have doubted such a thing was even possible if Audrey had not told me of this unusual experience. Audrey often had communication from God, but she didn't always tell me in what way it came to her.

—⁓—

Audrey, 1966

Audrey was eager to start a family though Aubrey Dean was reluctant to give up their freedom to enjoy fun-filled weekends of going places and doing things. When Audrey became pregnant, Aubrey Dean refused to talk with her about the baby. This was the beginning of sorrows for Audrey. During the sixth month of pregnancy, she went into labor, and the baby was born at the hospital around February 20, 1966. She was told that she had given birth to a baby boy, but she was not permitted to see him. Audrey had planned to name him Rodney Dewayne.

The stillborn baby was shown to Aubrey Dean, and he told us later that it did not look as if it could be normal if it had lived. He didn't volunteer more information, and my family did not pry. The baby was buried in a cemetery in Newport a short time after the birth while Audrey was not able to be a part of the burial. A young neighbor lady from Tuckerman had come to the hospital with Audrey and accompanied Aubrey Dean to the cemetery for the burial. It all happened very quickly, and family members were not informed about it in time to see the baby or to participate in the burial.

After Audrey came home from the hospital, I spent a few days with her while she grieved for her stillborn son and recovered from his birth. Audrey told me she planned to have another baby right away. She stated to me, "Every day that I'm not pregnant, my life is wasted."

What a strange thing to say, I thought. Not knowing how to respond to such a statement, I kept quiet. I wanted to tell her that it was not a good idea to plan another pregnancy so soon. I wished to tell her that her worth was not dependant on whether or not she has a child.

Blood tests showed that Audrey's blood was RH negative, and the baby's blood was positive. If the doctors had known in time, they could have taken measures to keep her body from rejecting the baby.

———

The Bufford Family

Sam was the son of a "preacher man" and farm laborer who went away to search for work in the big cities during the 1950s and again in the mid-1960s. Sam was the oldest of the nine Bufford children. As a young man in his teen years, Sam shared the enormous responsibility with his mother for the care of the household while his dad worked out of state. Several days would go by while his family waited for their share of the paycheck to come in the mail.

Mabel Margaret Motes Bufford

As a youth, Sam had taken jobs mowing lawns for four families in the rural communities near Grubbs and where he lived at Pitts. While privileged children went home to milk and cookies, Sam got off the school bus at a residence where he used their gasoline and push mower to cut the grass. He could smell the homeowners' supper cooking on the stove each time he made the return lap with the mower in the direction of the house. All his lawn care jobs were a couple of miles or more apart and required a long trek to his home at the end of the day. This extraordinary feat was all the more remarkable for the fact that Sam was a polio survivor and walked with a limp.

Sam had no true childhood. Even before he was old enough to perform manual labor, he was expected to tend the babies. In those days, babies wore cloth diapers that were pinned on with a large safety pin. Sam remembers on one occasion that he accidently pinned a diaper to the flesh of his little sister, Shirley, who was a squirming toddler and refused to lie still. He was pleased when he could turn that babysitting job over to Angie, who was the next oldest child in their large family, so he could go to the fields to work.

As a teenager, Sam occasionally went walking along the highway with his little sisters and brothers to retrieve soda pop bottles from the snake-infested road ditches to be redeemed for gasoline money. A small amount of money, less than two dollars, could buy enough gasoline to drive to church on Sunday. The church at Harmony Grove was such

Walking with God in the Backwoods

a comfortable place to be, for in the presence of the Lord, there was liberty and freedom from self-consciousness. Little country churches gave a sense of community to those who attended regularly. Each person had a sense of belonging and the privilege of being a part of something as grand as the family of God where other believers were their brothers and sisters in Christ.

Relationships were formed there with others of the same persuasion who enjoyed being accepted by people of the same economic disadvantage. Acceptance was a priceless treasure, which poor people found in God's house.

—m—

The Bufford Family Moves Away

In 1966, Sam's dad found work in the Detroit area and sent for his family. Sam assisted his mother as they packed and loaded their most valued belongings into a pickup truck to be driven by his Uncle Parm and Aunt Mae, with their three children who were more experienced travelers. Sam followed in an old station wagon with his mother and his eight siblings. Uncle Parm and Aunt Mae alternated driving their truck but Sam's mother did not have a license to drive. That left the responsibility for driving the second automobile to Sam alone. It was hot, and they were crowded and miserable. At rest stops, they could make a pallet on the grass and sleep for a few hours and let the children run about. Like a convoy, driving slower and making frequent stops, the trip from Pitts, Arkansas, to their new location in Taylor, Michigan, required that Sam drive thirty-six hours over the road.

After Sam's family moved to Michigan, we wrote long letters that drew us even closer than spoken words had before. Though Sam spent his childhood in the South, he did not have the privilege of enjoying leisure and forms of recreation. He had not been privileged to enjoy the sport of fishing and had never been deer hunting. Sam and I shared a common upbringing and had similar memories of childhood struggles. He could relate to the poverty in my family background and to the strength of my religious convictions. Together, we determined to change the course of our lives and in effect, the lives of generations to come.

—∞—

Drafted

Shortly after the Bufford family moved to Michigan, Sam was drafted into the army. He made the army medical personnel aware that he had a slight limp as a result of having had polio when he was little, but they ignored him. Most likely, every young man who had been drafted expressed a reasonable excuse by which he could be disqualified from serving in the military. Many American soldiers were being killed in Vietnam and many who survived were left disabled and emotionally handicapped. Many of Sam's loved ones were

Walking with God in the Backwoods

concerned and prayed faithfully for his safety. After Sam had been in boot camp for eight weeks, his commanding officer pulled him out of formation and asked why he was limping. Sam told him, "I have always limped, ever since I was two years old and had polio."

"Tomorrow you go and report to medical," the officer told Sam. When Sam arrived at medical the next morning, they presented him with a proposition. He could stay in the army and be assigned to a desk job or he could take a medical discharge and go home. Sam was homesick and quickly accepted the medical discharge. There was such rejoicing when the Bufford family discovered that Sam would be spared from going into combat.

Having contracted the dreaded polio as a small child was the very thing God used to keep Sam from the possibility of being sent to war. God was being merciful back then when his parents could hardly see that God was watching out for their child. But they continued to trust the Lord year after year, and they found Him to be faithful.

Graduation, 1967

Audrey had become a mother at the age of nineteen, just two months before my graduation. She arrived at our house with her new baby, Karen, to attend the ceremony. Audrey was instantly drawn into the chaos of preparations revolving around my significant event. Mama had recently cut my honey-blond hair to shoulder length, and I was not accustomed to the new style. Audrey was a capable person, and with her help, my hair would be fixed just right.

Since becoming teenagers, we had discovered that no one would guess how poor we were if we kept clean and neat and had nice hair. Audrey was a strawberry blond, but she would become annoyed if anyone mistook her for being a redhead, though our own dad had red hair. We washed our hair once a week in a round porcelain dishpan and filled another pan of the same size with water to rinse our hair. Adding vinegar to the rinse water not only made our hair shine but it decrease the possibility of getting head lice. Our family did not experience head lice while growing up though others in our school might have. When acquaintances remember the Motes girls, they usually think of "hair" because we had lots of it and tried to keep it looking nice.

Audrey was especially pleased that I was graduating because she had dropped out of school after the tenth grade. She had few regrets about having quit school, but she was glad that I had chosen not to do the same.

Noticing that the time had slipped away, I gathered my purse and cap and gown as Audrey and I prepared to join the family in the kitchen for supper. I informed my mother, "I have to be there early."

Mama had a meal on the table, but with this turn of events, we hardly had time to eat. It was my mother's habit to have a sit-down meal three times a day, and she saw to it that the dishes were washed immediately after each meal. (She had concerns about dirty dishes drawing ants, flies, and cockroaches.) If Mama did not have time to wash her dishes, she did not go. Without emotion, we were told to go on without her; she and the younger ones would stay home. Mama valued education and was pleased that I would be receiving a diploma, but she chose not to go. We did not discuss the incident that preceded the ceremony. I felt bad that I had not given her adequate foreknowledge, and had not helped with the cooking and dishwashing as I should have.

Mama had calmness of spirit and refused to be hurried. She avoided stressful situations and never overcommitted herself outside the home. We knew that we should not expect her to perform beyond her comfortable routine. The decision to skip my graduation did not wound me in any way. I was confident that I was loved, and she did not have to prove it with her attendance. This particular aspect of Eva's personality would not be easily understood by others, but Mama did not allow herself to be concerned about it.

Weiner was a farming community with a small population, the majority of which were hardworking and clean-living people. It was a place where most teenagers honored their parents and a time when most parents were honorable. My parents rarely received the honor they deserved, and I was not one to say complimentary words to them. I was pleased that our senior yearbook was dedicated to our parents with a full-page list of the parent's names, saying,

> We, the seniors of 1967, dedicate our yearbook to our parents whose loyalty, patience, and guidance have been a very great inspiration to all of us throughout our school years. As we finish our school career and go out to face the problems of tomorrow, we say, "Thank you, parents, for everything."

Feeling Free

Elvis Presley and Pricilla were newly married when I graduated on May 15, 1967. It seemed strange to be getting married so near the same time that they did. They were so rich and famous, yet they would be "newlyweds," and so would we.

Each of the forty-three graduates in the yearbook had chosen a motto, and it was printed beneath their senior picture. Some mottos were funny, and some were serious as each person attempted to give a word picture that would best reflect their personality. The six words that portrayed the longings of my heart were "Succeed: I can and I must." What appeared outwardly to be great ambition was probably more akin to inner discontent, for I was neither willing nor prepared to work hard at a career.

I was eager to enjoy the freedom to leave home immediately after the graduation ceremony. I rode with Audrey to her house to spend my last week in Arkansas before moving to Michigan and getting married. Audrey enjoyed being a wife, a mother, and a homemaker. She spent much of her alone time reading, sewing gifts for others and making quilts. Audrey and I went shopping for a pattern and white fabric that would be appropriate for sewing a simple wedding dress on her sewing machine. I chose to make a two-piece outfit with a straight skirt and a simple top with cap sleeves.

Audrey and I had been close all our life. She was more than a sister and more than a friend. She was like a little mother to all her siblings. I had never known life without her being there for me. She and I would never again be living in the same state. From this point on, our time together would be limited. We had no way of knowing how limited.

Lightening Out of Israel

On the same weekend we were married, there was "lightning out of Israel" as the Arab-Israeli conflict erupted into a war on June 4, 1967, which shook the spiritual world. The Jewish people, who had been dispersed all over the world, with millions of their people killed during the Holocaust, have shown the world that they are a powerful nation. Great and mighty things happened quickly that proved to all that God was with Israel. In a mere six days, the war ended with the Israeli army rejoicing in victory. Israel had obtained control of Jerusalem for the first time in close to two thousand years. Could this mean that the time of the Gentiles was being fulfilled?

> And they shall fall by the edge of the sword, and shall be led away captive into all nations: and Jerusalem shall be trodden down of the Gentiles, until the times of the Gentiles be fulfilled. (Luke 21:24)

Have the Gentiles declined significantly since that time? It appears that we have declined in power to win wars, in our

Walking with God in the Backwoods

economy with evidence of overwhelming debt, and spiritually as shown by the decline in our morals and the increase in violence.

In the Middle East, peace has been illusive, and fighting continues because hatred is a spirit and spirits do not die. At the end of our age, the spirit of hatred toward Jesus, the Son of God, will manifest in a man who will present himself as a man of peace, but in reality, he will be the Anti-Christ. (The Associated Press. *Lightning Out of Israel: The Arab-Israeli Conflict*. Commemorative edition. Racine: Western Printing and Lithographing Company, 1967.)

Tuckerman, Arkansas, 1968

The year after I moved to Michigan, Audrey became weak and sickly, and the doctor in Newport did not seem to know what to do for her. She eventually went to Erlene's doctor in Memphis to be checked. The doctor there said he thought she had high blood pressure and suspected that she might be diabetic. It was such a long distance that she could not easily make the three-hour trip for more tests and follow-up visits.

My parents moved their family of five to a two-bedroom home in the small town of Tuckerman in 1968 when Joe, Mildred, and Andrew were teenagers. Meanwhile, another family occupied the farmhouse. Joe graduated from Tuckerman High School which was about two miles from

Mabel Margaret Motes Bufford

Audrey and Aubrey Dean's home in the country. With help from Joe and Andrew, my father farmed in the area. During the time they lived in town, they were relieved of cutting and carrying firewood and pumping and carrying water. Grandma West went to live with them for a year before she had to go to a nursing home. Grandma was suffering from the broken hip that would not heal, and Audrey was often sick. With family members living close by, each watched out for the other.

During the summer while Mildred was fifteen years of age, she went home from church with a girl friend who introduced her to a neighbor boy, William (Bill) Mount. In the fall, Mildred attended the Tuckerman High School and saw him every day at school. He became one of Andrew's new friends and came to visit in their home often. Though Mildred was painfully shy and could hardly talk to boys, she and Bill liked each other right away. After being friends and going together for two years, they talked of spending their whole life together. There was no dating as others know it, for there was no money and no place to go.

—∿—

Mildred, 1970

Both Mildred and Bill Mount chose not to go back to school in the fall of 1970 and made plans to get married.

When all arrangements had been finalized to rent a house in town, Mildred and Bill walked casually next door

Walking with God in the Backwoods

to the pastor's house and had the simplest wedding ceremony possible in his living room.

The dress Mildred wore for the ceremony was nothing special, just a cotton dress that she had worn for the last two terms of school. There was no reception of any kind, not even cake and punch. When the ceremony was over, they simply went to their own place. Bill had turned eighteen the month before, and Mildred would turn eighteen the month after the wedding. In spite of such humble beginnings, Mildred and Bill have been together forty-five years as of 2015.

It was a desire of my mother's heart that her daughters not feel the hurt and rejection that she had experienced in her youth. Eva had suffered poverty and discrimination when she was a single mother, so she prayed for a good husband for each of her girls. God answered her prayer and brought the mate of His choice.

—⟡—

The Warning, 1970

While doing mundane housework on an ordinary day, I had an unusual experience. As I was walking from the bedroom, in my mind, I saw a blank screen with words going across it slowly like the tornado warnings going across a television screen when a severe storm is approaching. I slowed my hurried pace immediately so I could read the words. After I took a couple more slow steps, the words stopped moving.

Choosing to come to a complete halt, the word began to move again. I stood still while reading. I had never heard of this happening before to anyone, but I knew it was a spiritual experience—a message was coming directly from the Holy Spirit of God.

As I continued to read, I realized this was a funeral sermon. I wondered aloud as if talking to God without using words, "Am I supposed to be writing this down?" There was no answer, but the words kept moving slowly. I began talking to myself with thoughts like, *I am not a preacher, and no one is going to ask me to preach a sermon. There is no need for me to write down a funeral sermon.*

Berating thoughts began to come to me, *Margaret, you are really losing it.* With my thoughts causing interference, the words stopped. Then I saw a full-screen picture of many automobiles in a long funeral procession. Immediately, I thought of my dad. *This must be happening because my father is becoming old and his hard job with farm machinery is often dangerous.* The troubling message stopped, and I put it out of my thoughts as I went on with my housework. I didn't have to wait long to know whose life was in the balance, for a phone call came from Audrey within hours.

Audrey, Fall of 1970

Audrey had continued to visit her doctor in Newport, and he sent her to the hospital in Little Rock for more tests. Before the Thanksgiving holiday in 1970, when Audrey had turned twenty-three, she was diagnosed with kidney failure. Her doctor told her that she was not going to recover, and she had one month to live. That was such unexpected and shocking news for Audrey and Aubrey Dean. I was not told how they reacted upon being informed of the seriousness of Audrey's condition and her impending death. I did not ask, and neither was I told how they handled it when they were finally left alone. Within a couple hours, they arrived home from the hospital and began the difficult task of passing the information along to the immediate family first and then to closest friends and then to the neighbors. Like blows from a hammer, those words being said over and over drove the reality of their situation home to them. When Audrey called me with the devastating news, my exact words were, "Oh, Audrey, what are you going to do?"

"I guess I'll just pray and trust God. That's all I can do," she answered. I could not accept the finality of this news and rejected the prophetic warning God had given me. My first impulse was to do something to reverse her death sentence. I suggested to Audrey that I could come to Arkansas and give her one of my kidneys. In the next few days, Audrey phoned her doctor and informed him that a family member wanted to be checked for the possibility of being a kidney donor, but Audrey's blood type would be harder to match. Audrey needed frequent blood transfusions because her kidneys could not filter her blood adequately. Though an adult, Mildred was disqualified as a blood donor because she weighed a mere eighty-three pounds. Joe was disqualified as a blood donor for his blood pressure was too high. I traveled from Michigan to Arkansas to be examined and had a tissue test done to see if I could donate a kidney. Our blood type was the same, but she was negative and I was positive. I stayed with Audrey for two weeks and then went back home to wait for word from her to let me know when I should come back for her surgery.

Audrey was seriously ill and needed Mildred's help in tending her three-year-old child, Karen. Audrey had been like a second mother to Mildred, and Mildred in turn was like a second mother to Karen. Audrey had kidney dialysis treatments once a week, leaving for the hospital on Sunday afternoon and returning home on Wednesday evening. Aubrey Dean would drive her to the hospital one hundred miles away and leave her so he could continue working at the body shop in Newport. Mildred made herself available to watch Karen while Audrey was gone to the hospital and to sit with Audrey during her days at home and help with her child care and household responsibilities.

1971

It was such a blessing that Mama and Daddy got to live near Audrey and her family for three years. Those few years in Tuckerman brought Mildred alongside Audrey to help her through the most difficult time of her life. It also brought Mildred to the mate of God's choice.

In the new year of 1971, Mama and Daddy chose to move back to the farm where the house had become vacant. Joe went with them to help farm, but Andrew stayed in Tuckerman with Mildred and Bill to finish the school term so he could graduate with his class.

It was so hard for Audrey to get answers from the doctors. I suppose they did not want to take away her hope, but they couldn't go forward. Like the ebb tide, Audrey's life was slipping away; time was running out, and I could not be there for her. A life-saving operation was never scheduled, and she continued to become weaker. Audrey died alone at the University of Arkansas Hospital in Little Rock on April 14, 1971, at the age of twenty-three. She had managed to live four months longer than the doctor had predicted. Left behind was a young husband with their little daughter, Karen, who was four years old. With Audrey's death, I became the oldest girl in our family and inherited her role of big sister. It was then that I realized why Audrey's role was not prominent in the prophetic dream I had years ago, which predicted Kathy's future, Audrey's future, and my future.

Mabel Margaret Motes Bufford

The dogwoods were in bloom when Sam and I drove to Arkansas for Audrey's funeral at the Assembly of God Church in Tuckerman. I was amazed to hear that Audrey had been in church on Easter Sunday, just three days before she died. The last Sunday school lesson and the last sermon she heard was about the resurrection. Of all the sermons she could have heard, that one was probably the most comforting. Audrey left a legacy of faithfulness to God which is being recorded for future generations in Motes family history.

While they were only eighteen, Mildred and Bill were endowed with the wisdom and maturity necessary to take Karen into their home and give her a sense of security and stability. The kind young man that God had chosen to be Mildred's husband worked full-time and helped her to care for the motherless child in his free time.

After nine months, Aubrey Dean brought a young woman to Mildred's house and introduced her as his new wife. He was eager to be a husband and a father once again. Five-year-old Karen gathered her belongings immediately, for she was excited to go to live with her father and new stepmother in the house that had once been her home. Aubrey Dean loved Karen, and she loved him. Mildred and I visited Karen there on one occasion while I was vacationing in Arkansas. Soon afterward, Aubrey Dean and his new wife moved to Texas, and our family did not see Karen again for about four years.

It is sad that when we lost Audrey, we lost Aubrey Dean, and when he remarried and moved away, we lost Karen for

Walking with God in the Backwoods

a while. The house where they had lived burned down a few years afterward. Not only was Audrey and her whole little family taken away from us, but even the house that they had purchased when it was newly built ceased to exist. It was as if the enemy of Audrey's soul wanted all evidence erased that she had ever existed. Later, I understood why Audrey had been so determined to give birth to a child. It was important for her to leave a part of herself in this world.

> So teach us to number our days,
> that we may apply our hearts unto wisdom.
>
> —Psalms 90:12

I'll Meet You in the Morning
1994

WHILE ON VACATION AT MY parents' tiny house in Bradford, Arkansas, I lay in bed and remembered how things used to be when I was a kid. Marvelous memories were created in the 1950s; it was a time when the pace of life was painstakingly slow. Each day dawned with the strutting and crowing competition between dueling roosters bent on proving their importance. Indoors, the morning ritual began with the abrupt striking of a match for lighting a kerosene lamp. The momentary smell of sulfur was a gentle, aromatic wake-up call. My parents, Levi and Eva, were up long before daylight, often as early as four o'clock in the morning. A fire had to be built in the wood-burning cook stove before breakfast could be prepared. It would take near an hour before they could have a fire that was hot enough to heat the blackened pot full of water for hot coffee and a thick cast-iron skillet for frying eggs. Starting time in the fields for a farmer and his hired help was at six o'clock sharp. Rarely did a farmer sleep in; it would just be unthinkable.

Daddy, a spry little man, was as quick as a bantam rooster. He was a happy man who had great faith in God. Daddy did not seem to mind working hard, and he did not appear to worry about anything. He enjoyed farm life and caring for the animals. Being eager to get outside, he would check on the barnyard animals a hundred feet or so beyond the outhouse. Farmers did not spend much time inside the house except at night and mealtimes. A hardworking, tractor-driving man did not need anything fancy just for sleeping and eating. The house was mostly for the women and the children. Daddy whistled joyfully as he walked at a brisk pace. Returning with a bucket of water from the hand pump, he gave an assessment of our state of affairs. He gave the daily weather and livestock report to Mama while washing his hands in the wash pan that sat next to the water bucket. He was a positive person and pleasant to be with.

—◊◊◊—

When I Was Young

One of the most appreciated things among the women and children was the convenience of a chamber pot or "pee-pot" in the bedroom. It afforded us the luxury of avoiding the walk in the darkness and fearing snakes in the grass. Even in the summer, it was too cold for the women and children to use an outhouse before daylight. The little boys enjoyed the advantage of being able to pee off the front porch in the darkness.

On the farm, women did not complain about being treated differently than a man. There was no advantage in fighting with the men of the family for equality. For both men and women, the battle was with the poverty that enslaved all of us. We needed each other—just to make life bearable. We valued every distinctive measure taken to assure that our lives would be made easier, and we honored the man who concerned himself with our state of being.

Mixing biscuit dough each morning; Mama took flour from a fifty-pound barrel and lard from a bucket which we called "a stand of lard." Eva was a slow-moving person but managed to accomplish a lot—only because she plodded along at a steady pace. That was her secret to being a successful farm wife—she was never idle. When she needed to rest, she wrote letters, read newspapers, or took a nap. She was always doing something.

Daddy sat leisurely at the table and talked as Mama spread melted grease on top of the biscuits before placing them in the oven. Breakfast always consisted of biscuits and eggs, of which we had plenty. Often, there would be white milk gravy in which to sop the biscuits. If we were fortunate enough to have a cow for milking, there would be sweet milk and fresh churned butter. When there was no cow to give milk, we used evaporated milk for cooking. Our parents drank coffee for breakfast, but if there was no milk for the children, we drank tea or Kool-Aid for breakfast.

Lingering over steaming hot coffee and comforted by the warmth of a crackling fire, Levi and Eva engaged in conversation as true friends—just visiting. I knew they loved each other, though they never said it. I got up early one morning desiring to join in the magic of their closeness, but it seemed to break the spell. I concluded that it was more comforting to lie in bed—snuggled under a pile of quilts—and listen to the rise and fall of their voices. It gave me a sense of security knowing that they valued their special time as they shared the freshness and beauty of daybreak. Otherwise, the house was totally quiet as the dimness of night gave way to hues of pink on a gray sky and the wink of a rising sun.

—∞—

Visiting My Elderly Parents

My parents were empowered by their vivid memories of hardships and by a rigid work ethic. They lived alone and cared for themselves in the small town of Bradford, where they had access to all the modern conveniences. At the age of eighty-three, my father produced enough vegetables in his garden each year to supply a large family. He went hunting for the wild game they ate, and he cut his own firewood to

Walking with God in the Backwoods

heat the house. My mother did the canning and freezing of fruits and vegetables that were raised on their large lot in town. Those things just did not change.

While visiting my parents, I became aware of the changes in me and in Sam since our childhood. I made it a point to rise early and enjoyed my parents around the breakfast table. Being extremely tired, Sam was eager to sleep in after traveling sixteen hours to reach our destination. My dad was under the impression that no man should sleep in; it was not the manly thing to do. If farmers needed extra sleep, they just went to bed early—"with the chickens." Sam had worked the night shift most of his years in the automobile factory, and my father had little understanding of that routine. Daddy tried to understand. He just could not change his childlike impatience for waiting on a sleeping man—and his dislike for it.

"Hey, city boy," Daddy called out to Sam, teasing him with fiendish delight. "It's time to get up." In a good-natured way, he recited a list of chores he had accomplished while Sam had slept. Sam played along with the game and was coaxed out of bed with the promise of a cup of hot coffee.

Daddy liked to act as a tour guide and showed off everything he had grown in various places on the two-acre lot in Bradford. I noticed that Daddy had two gardens—one on each side of the creek. It was his nature to give vegetables to the elderly, the needy, and to the pastor of the church. But two gardens are just too much for two elderly people. I asked

Mabel Margaret Motes Bufford

him why he had two gardens. As he pointed across the ditch, he said, "That one is for the rabbits. If I let them eat that one, then maybe they'll leave this one alone."

Being exceptionally good at gardening, Daddy was always eager to get started each spring. He often planted potatoes too early, around the first week of February, and many times, the freezing weather killed the tops of the potatoes, and they had to come up again from the root. There was furious competition as Daddy competed with Mike to see which of them could grow the biggest and the best vegetables.

Around February 14, Daddy planted lettuce, cabbage, radishes, beats, and English peas in his early garden. With such a long growing season in Arkansas, he managed to have not only an early garden but also a later garden. Around April 15, Daddy planted tomatoes, corn, all kinds of beans, watermelons, and sweet potatoes. His late garden was planted around the last of August and consisted of mustard greens and turnip greens which he called his "salet patch."

During my visit, there was something Daddy needed from the store, so I hopped in his battered pickup truck to go with him. On the seat between us lay an old black bible. It had been patched with gray duct tape for such a long time that dirt had stuck to the glue around the edges of the tape. I could hardly believe the condition of the bible and the neediness it implied. As I picked it up, I said, "Oh, Daddy, let me buy you another bible."

"Oh no, I have a good bible that I carry to church," he said. "This is just the one I carry in the truck." I knew Daddy had not learned to read well, and I was surprised that he read a King James Bible enough to wear it out. Mama had always done all the reading aloud to him. His favorite verse was John 1:1. He would quote it proudly as if he was quoting poetry. I suspected that he had heard that verse and many other scriptures often enough to memorize them and taught himself to read the words.

Later that day, Mama and I were talking in the kitchen and preparing dinner, I commented about how poor we were while I was growing up. I happened to be looking at her face, and I could see that she was both surprised and offended. In a stern tone that set the record straight, she said, "You were never poor. You always had plenty to eat."

At that moment, I was enlightened to the fact that my parents never thought they were impoverished. They were grateful to God for everything they owned and content with what they had. I suppose each person has their own version of poverty—what they interpret it to be or what they compare it to.

—⟡—

Rising Early

Somehow, the farmer's philosophy and work ethic escaped my grasp. As a child, I struggled to function underneath the

Mabel Margaret Motes Bufford

weight of self-imposed guilt that it produced in me. I was of the serious and sedentary sort. I still do not enjoy physical activities and manual labor as much as some people do.

I got a letter from my youngest brother, Andrew, saying he has been getting up very early for years and starting his work at three thirty each morning. I was forty-four years old before I could boast of rising at 4:30 a.m. six days a week. I think I have derived as much pleasure from that accomplishment as from any other. I have been released from the sense of guilt of having failed to achieve my parents' standard. What time I choose to get out of bed, in Michigan, is of no interest to my parents now. I have no reason to discuss it or to give an account. Having achieved the standard, I find that it is of no importance to anyone—except to me—and is profitable only for my own satisfaction.

> From the rising of the sun unto the going down of the same the LORD's name is to be praised.
>
> —Psalms 113:3

16

This World Is Not My Home

Winter comes early here in Columbiaville, Michigan; by late October, the leaves are off the trees. The beauty of autumn has been tucked away in our memory folder and filed in the past. The trees look similar to telephone poles surrounded by lifeless giant sticks. The year is almost gone.

The house was suddenly quiet as my teenage children, Sammy and Krista, walked out the front door and headed for the bus stop. A sense of loneliness engulfed me. It was a cold, dreary November morning with a cold rain dampening the outdoors and my spirit as well.

It seems that nature insists on an extended pause during November to make a set change between performances. Like an impatient child, my enthusiasm wanes during intermission as I view an empty gray stage between the scenes of autumn's color change and the magnificent scenic wonder of winter's snow.

I feel guilty for allowing myself to be so affected by the absence of sunshine. I also feel guilty for not being prone to see beauty in this stage of nature's cycle of seasons. My state of mind depends largely on the sunshine and the beauty of nature. For this reason, I mourn the passing of summer as if it were the death of an old friend. Autumn leaves are magnificent in their fiery brilliance, but I view them as I do the floral display at the funeral home; their beauty is diminished by the reminder that a painful good-bye is eminent.

—m—

The Premonition, 1994

The first snow of the season produced a "snow day" and thrilled the school children with a holiday in which to celebrate the onset of winter. Yet with the fickleness of a young lady, Mother Nature changed her mind and decreed the Christmas holiday of 1994 would be long remembered for having the mildest weather in recent records. I determined to enjoy the unexpected respite, knowing that we would soon be battling the elements—the bitter cold and howling winds that attempt annually to turn our snow-covered landscape into a vast frozen wasteland.

"We're having an Arkansas Christmas," I concluded, for there was no snowfall anywhere in the state of Michigan. I chuckled to myself as I remembered how the old-timers in

Walking with God in the Backwoods

the Southern backwoods could tell you in which year was the "drought," which one was the year of the "high water," and in which year we had the "ice over." In their mind, it held enormous significance, second only to the importance of great historic events such as the Great Depression.

I scooped up the mail from the rural-type mailbox at the street and walked briskly to the house with the satisfaction of a greedy pirate eager to examine his precious jewels. With anticipation, I thumbed through the Christmas cards and was delighted to find one from my elderly parents. I knew at a glance which cards were sure to have a letter enclosed, which ones would have a friendly note, and which ones would have a stoic signature. Mentally, I placed the cards in the order that I would open them, leaving the best until last. Mama's card, guaranteed to have a letter, would be savored like a rare delicacy.

I enjoy getting mail. It almost ruins my day if I go to the mailbox only to find it as barren as a languishing soul. So much of who I am was forged in a childhood of poverty and isolation where the most dependable link to the outside world was the mail carrier. He was the poor families' version of Santa Claus.

I laid the mail on the dining-room table only as long as it took to throw my coat over a chair. I could endure the suspense no longer and proceeded to tear into the Christmas cards. The card from my parents displayed an old-fashioned candlelight scene, with a lone violin and a single page of timeworn sheet music. *This looks like the type of card my mother would choose*, I thought.

It does not, I protested immediately, as if there was another entity inside my head. *There is no musical talent in our family at all.* I stared at the card, surprised that it had so captivated me. I perceived sadness in this particular scene as if an occasion of heavenly communion had been interrupted—causing a much-loved instrument to be abandoned and allowing no time to blow out the candle. I was getting a premonition. I felt a strange sense of knowing—my mother would die first. *This card I should save*, I thought. *It could be the last Christmas card I'll get from my mother.*

My mother is old, but then she has always seemed old to me. I was born when she was in her mid-thirties. Her life experiences have spanned many decades of technological advances. Her memories invoke the infancy of all the modern conveniences that we now consider to be necessities. I am surprised that I am just now having thoughts about the reality of her age—eighty-one. I am made acutely aware of the inevitable process of aging as the dread of finality intrudes into my thoughts. Having a premonition is very distressing, though I do appreciate an early warning, and I do need time to prepare myself.

As I taped Mama's Christmas card over the doorway for display, I instinctively stepped through an imaginary threshold that separates the bliss of youthful naïveté into the insightfulness of middle age. It is too painful to consider the possibility of my mother's impending death, so I struggle to put it out of my thoughts.

—∽—

Depression

Cabin fever is a term they use in the North for the condition of extreme loneliness and boredom as a result of being "snowed in" and isolated. During those times, I longed to live near my extended family in the South. There was no hope that they would choose to live near me in Michigan. So I clung to the hope of returning to my home state of Arkansas when Sam retired.

The term *seasonal affective depression disorder* (SADD) was unfamiliar to me until I was older. Finally, there was a label for the depressed mood I suffered during the long winter months indoors. I believe my mother suffered from this malady, which is made worse by loneliness, isolation, and a lack of social skills.

After many years with a diminished quality of life, I went to a psychologist who helped to get me back on track by teaching me how to combat the negative self-talk. For immediate relief, he recommended an antidepressant—Prozac; it helped, but not enough. The medication was changed to Wellbutrin. With Wellbutrin, I saw a greater improvement. While sitting in a rocking chair, I rocked. While working, I hummed. It took a few years for me to "wing it" on my own without medication.

Mabel Margaret Motes Bufford

The next time I was on vacation in Arkansas, I confided to Mildred that I was on an antidepressant. She told me that one of her grown children had been on antidepressants. She had been reluctant to share that information with anyone because of the stigma attached to depression. I felt bad that she feared my reaction if she should dare to tell me.

I told one of my brothers about me being on antidepressants, and he confided that he too had struggled to combat depression. It saddened me to know that someone I love has suffered in silence due to the shame and embarrassment of depression. With research, I discovered there were supplements which help to alleviate some of the suffering: fish oil or flaxseed oil, vitamin D, folic acid and the B vitamins, and tryptophan. In addition to supplements, I needed more exercise and more time in the sunshine. With journaling and having a daily devotional regimen, I got through the emotional hurdles—change of life and adjusting to the empty nest.

The psychologist said it is possible that my mother suffered from untreated depression during portions of her adult life as well. I can remember my mother buying a bottle of cod liver oil in an attempt to solve her problem with a depressed mood. "Fish is brain food," she read aloud from a magazine article. (We rarely ate fish.) It seems that people in regions of the world where fish is consumed more frequently do suffer less depression. At that time, cod liver oil was the supplement for people who did not have access to fresh fish.

Walking with God in the Backwoods

My mother had gone through a complete hysterectomy without taking any replacement hormones. She battled tremendous hardship, grief, and depression without the aid of antidepressants. She survived with little help or encouragement from family, friends, or neighbors. If it wasn't the cod liver oil that helped her to survive, then it must have been by the grace of God, for that was all she had. I have been blessed to have strong women in my family as role models. All of them were stronger than I have become.

Growing Old, 1995

The inevitable has happened. Magazine articles that once merited a casual glance, like "financial planning" and "growing old gracefully," are now topics of interest to me. My husband, Sam, is accepting the evidence of aging much better than I am. Until our four children became teenagers, *old* was a term that applied to someone other than me. Nowadays, I get frequent reminders that I am out of step with the times. We were never *with it* when we were younger, so it should not bother me to be *over the hill* now. I do not know the current terms well enough to know if I am still considered *square* or if I would qualify as *a stick in the mud*. Either of those terms would be much kinder, I must admit, than the old-fashioned term *fuddy-duddy*.

Mabel Margaret Motes Bufford

"I wish you guys had been hippies at Woodstock. Then, you could have been cool," said our youngest child, fifteen-year-old daughter, Krista. As parents, we are somewhat of a disappointment to our children. Our lack of cool is what they consider to be a handicap to themselves. Our second oldest child, twenty-year-old daughter, Shelia, said her dad and I have more in common with her friends' grandparents than with her friend's parents.

I have not attained sufficient sophistication to be endowed with a sense of belonging; I no longer expect it. While growing up on the farm, I did not sense that I belonged there either. At that time, it was my goal to blend in with everyone else at school and to avoid drawing attention to myself. While suffering from shyness and self-consciousness, I rarely had a sense of acceptance from people in any public place— except church. I felt totally accepted by God and perfectly comfortable in His presence.

When we go back to visit in Arkansas, we find that things are modern and that our childhood memories have no place to call home. Sometimes, it seems as if the world Sam and I experienced as youngsters is as far removed as if it happened on another planet.

As a child, my religious training had been reinforced in Gospel songs, and I enjoyed singing. The message of hope in those old hymns encouraged us to fix our eyes on a goal beyond this world. When we sang "I'll Fly Away," our spirits soared to heavenly places. From such lofty heights, we could

Walking with God in the Backwoods

see life from a new perspective. Commitments were made to God and to family while we sang "When the Roll Is Called Up Yonder," for we planned to be there. We could see clearly the path before us. We had plenty of dreams and noble aspirations, for they were free of cost. We knew where we wanted to go in life and had the confidence that we would get there, simply because God was with us.

"This World Is Not My Home" was the title of an old Gospel hymn that expressed my sense of alienation as a child from the backwoods. "I'm jest ah passen' through," I sang with gusto as my thoughts turned back to the first time I was aware of the feelings of not belonging.

Misconceptions

The picture of a baby wrapped in a diaper and being delivered by a stork in flight was a trademark that was seen often on baby products and in magazine ads during the 1950s. As a little girl, I saw the emblem and asked my mother what the bird was doing with that baby. She explained what the symbol implied. The conversation progressed to the point of my asking, "Is that how I got here?" She assured me that was the case—a stork brought me.

I could reason just enough that I asked, "Where does the stork get the babies?" Mama became uncomfortable with the direction of the conversation and ended it simply by choosing not to discuss it further. I was rather troubled about not knowing where I came from. "The stork must have taken me from *somewhere* or from *someone*," I reasoned. "Maybe I belong to another family, and the stork flying overhead stole me away from my true family." Occasionally, I would remember my dilemma as I had opportunity to observe other families in the waiting room at the doctor's office.

Could those people be my real family? I wondered as I observed pretty young mothers nurturing their dainty little girls with ivory skin. Even at a young age, I noticed that affluent children did not show as much evidence of having spent time in the hot sun as we did. I never saw any other family that I thought might be mine. As time went by, I realized that I was quite comfortable in this family, and there was to be no lingering thoughts of another. Still, it would be a long time before I would know the truth about my origin.

—✴—

Self-Acceptance

Our firstborn daughter, Michelle, has made me a granny with the birth of our first grandchild. It would be more exciting to be a grandparent if it didn't remind me that I'm getting old.

Sometimes, my four children tire of my reminiscing and begin to make fun of me. "I know, I know," Krista says, "you walked five miles to school every day, uphill both ways." Wistfully, I come back down to earth.

Walking with God in the Backwoods

I confided to a young man who was visiting in our home that I feel different from other people and just do not seem to belong anywhere. He assured me that being somewhat different was quite acceptable. "It adds variety and flare among the masses," he said. "I find it intriguing and refreshing to see displays of individuality."

"But I never wanted to be strange," I said, with disdain.

"Oh, you're not strange," he responded, attempting to be kind. "You're a little eccentric, maybe."

I have accepted the fact of my being different, but there is little comfort in being labeled eccentric.

Nothing but the Truth

My younger sister, Mildred, came to visit me from Possum Grape, Arkansas, accompanied by her daughter, Tina. Both ladies stand no more than five feet tall and weighed in the range of 110 pounds. Though these homegrown Southern gals are frail in appearance, they are of the Steel Magnolia variety. We are not only kin, but we are the best of friends. I always trust Mildred to tell me the truth in a gentle way to soften the blow to my self-esteem. I value her assessment of situations, for she is an intuitive person and possesses a great deal of wisdom. Mildred and I enjoy a depth of communication that ministers to the spirit and nourishes the soul. During one session of girl talk, we had an intense moment of emotional closeness and vulnerability. I told Mildred and Tina about my apprehensions. "Mildred," I said, as I leaned forward in a serious manner, "do you think I'm…strange?"

Before Mildred could answer my question, Tina blurted out, "I think you're both strange!" We erupted in unrestrained laughter. Mildred and I do seem to think differently than other women our ages. We've been like aliens in our own country as we tried to assimilate into a modern society. Maybe we were warped by life in the backwoods, or maybe we were enriched by it. Now, I have new problems with which to deal and me having failed to be *cool* is not one of them; neither is the dislike for being considered *old*. I must accept that I am perceived as *eccentric* and *strange*, but to my dismay, I was the last to know.

I am reminded of a quote I read, "The only normal people are those we don't know very well." It seems that everyone has a negative trait to battle or "a cross to bear." Only in our struggles can strength be obtained for godly character to shine forth. I am comforted by the fact that God loves me just the way I am. He knows what I am and what I am not, and He chose me anyway.

> For he knoweth our frame;
> he remembereth that we are dust.

—Psalms 103:14

Love Lifted Me

Aunt Mabel

I HAVE VERY FEW MEMORIES of my mother's youngest sister, Aunt Mabel, before she left home to go to college in a faraway city. I was only about five, but I remember the special bond and affection that is between a child and a loving aunt who is a single girl. Every child should have an aunt like my Aunt Mabel.

After Aunt Mabel West Earls became a wife, a mother, and a schoolteacher in California, she chose to stay involved in our life through occasional letters. She was a very generous person, and she surprised us with a package every few years. It gave us a sense of worth to be loved by a special person so far away. Though we rarely got to see her, she occupied a place of honor in our hearts. She was a celebrity in our little world, and her influence was powerful. Knowing that she thought of us and cared about us was very comforting and gave us a sense of security.

Aunt Mabel passed away at the age of seventy in the summer of 1994. My mother grieved terribly for the loss of her favorite sister who was also like a pen pal and best friend. I had written a note to Aunt Mabel for Mother's Day in 1985, and it was returned to me after her death when her personal items were being sorted.

Aunt Mabel

Thank you for being so good to your family.
You gave us love and hope and encouragement
That we sensed in every letter and card.
You were a great role model, an ideal,
Providing pleasant memories.
You were a gift from God.

You were proof that life could be better.
As a result, I dared to dream.
You overcame poverty and became "somebody."
Because of you I dared to hope.
As a gracious lady, you were a symbol of excellence.
Without your example,
I might never have dared to try.

Miss Myrth

Some names are so unusual, or seldom used, that only the first name is necessary to identify that notable person—names like Elvis, Cher, and Oprah are such names. Myrth is a unique name that suits a grand lady known to the people around Weiner, Arkansas, and in the community of Long Creek. Miss Myrth, now ninety-seven years old, has become a local celebrity. She said that a person, eighty years ago, could take a test to prove that they were capable of teaching and become a schoolteacher as soon as they finished high school.

Though Miss Myrth Howard's childhood home and farm was less than a mile behind the Long Creek school/church, the school was not equipped to educate students beyond the eighth grade. Arrangements were made for the young lady to stay at her uncle's house in town to complete her schooling and graduate from Weiner High School.

Having passed the test, Miss Myrth became a schoolteacher during the fall semester while she was still seventeen before turning eighteen on November 22. She taught at the Long Creek school/church for seven years. There was very little money paid to schoolteachers back then.

Planning a great adventure, Miss Myrth and her best girl friend from the community of Long Creek, Ocy Kinard, moved to an apartment in the big city of Memphis, Tennessee. Having no car, they traveled there by bus and rode about the city on a street car. Both young ladies got jobs at Fisher

Mabel Margaret Motes Bufford

Aircraft and did the job of "Rosie the Riveter" for a whole year. They had a grand time and earned much better wages than Miss Myrth had earned for teaching school in the country.

An interest in a former classmate from high school, Robert Hibbard, was the deciding factor in Miss Myrth returning to Arkansas. Robert had joined the navy and was involved in the heavy fighting at Guadalcanal during World War II. While exchanging letters, Robert expressed a desire for Miss Myrth to return to Arkansas and to her teaching career. Complying with his wishes, she quit her job and returned to the Long Creek community to arrange for a teaching job in the Grubbs School. After a year of teaching there and writing to Robert, he returned from the war. He had served for seven years in the navy before the two were married in 1944. Upon finishing the second year of teaching at Grubbs, she arranged to become the first-grade teacher at the Weiner Elementary School where most people have continued—even until this day—to call her Miss Myrth.

Miss Myrth was ten years older than her only sibling, E. G. Howard. The fact that everyone called the boy E. G. gave him a distinctive name that easily set him apart. He and his sister shared the notoriety of having unique names that were well-known in their part of the country.

When Audrey was small and I was a toddler, my father sharecropped for E. G. Howard, and we lived in the house that had been their childhood home. While living there, my parents attended the Long Creek Baptist church, and we rode in a wagon pulled by a team of mules to attend the Sunday services. My mother and Miss Myrth were longtime friends and stayed in touch for the rest of my mother's life. They enjoyed sharing the memories of people they knew long ago. Though Mama did not visit Miss Myrth, she wrote letters to her anytime there was news involving someone from their past. She sent news to Miss Myrth of the progress and achievements of people they both cared about. Miss Myrth did not have time to write letters, but she did come to visit every few years. One time, she brought a few handed-down dresses someone had donated for her to pass along to a needy family. The two friends often saw each other at the funerals of old acquaintances in the community.

—∿—

Miss Myrth's Memories

When I talked to Miss Myrth this July 2015, she told me that she remembers going with her mother and little brother, E. G., to visit my grandmother Della West near Grubbs. Miss Myrth's mother had been a friend of my grandmother for many years. She said when they arrived, my grandmother was making cupcakes, and it delighted little E. G. when Grandma West gave him a cupcake.

My great-grandmother, Delaiah Jane Clark, born in the 1860s, had been the midwife who cared for Mrs. Howard and helped to deliver little E. G. when he was born at home. My great-grandma had stayed at the Howard family's home for three months to care for Mrs. Howard before her baby was due and after the baby was born. Great-grandma Clark was so concerned about complications for her patient that she called for a doctor to be present for the home delivery.

Miss Myrth and her mother were very social people and seemed to know everyone. Miss Myrth also knew my grandparents, David and Mary, who sharecropped near Flag Slough. Mary passed away before Eva got to meet Levi and the Motes family but her friend, Miss Myrth, could tell her that "Mary was well liked and had a good name in the community." Though Mary Motes died eighty-one years ago, Miss Myrth knew her. When Miss Myrth was a young girl, she and the Motes family attended church together, and she was still there when Mr. Motes moved back to her area with grown sons. Miss Myrth not only knew my uncles, but she knew the girls from the Long Creek community that the boys married. She was acquainted with all six of Mary Motes' daughters-in-law. Not only had they attended church together, three of those girls had been among her students. When Hester, Uncle John Henry's wife, was buried a few years ago at the Clark cemetery, Miss Myrth and E. G. attended the graveside funeral of her former student.

Miss Myrth taught the first five of Uncle Jesse and Aunt Veelia's fourteen children at the Long Creek School and still sees some of them at the annual reunion. While teaching the first grade at Weiner Elementary, she taught five children belonging to Eva and Levi. That makes ten of Mary Motes' grandchildren that were taught by Miss Myrth.

It amazes me that my first-grade teacher knew both sets of my grandparents—David and Mary and Della West, who were born in the 1880s, and my grandfather Sam West, who was born in 1871. She knew many of my relatives that I never met. This makes her seem like family to me.

In 1970, Miss Myrth lost her husband of twenty-six years. Without having children of her own and the loss of both parents, the only relatives she had left were E. G., his wife, and his daughter, Teressa.

Miss Myrth genuinely loves people and enjoys hearing how families are connected one to the other in the community. By attending funerals, she and E. G. kept up with everybody that they once knew. Funerals were an event where they could see the people who moved away decades ago and were scattered all over our nation. In this way, they stayed connected and kept the sense of community alive for themselves and those involved in their lives. Miss Myrth has kept her mind sharp by remembering places and events while keeping the names of former students, old friends, and acquaintances fresh in her memory.

E. G. and Miss Myrth were always close; they were best of friends as well as brother and sister. Going for rides in the country was a favorite outing for the two of them. They enjoyed seeing the changes to the landscape as the construction projects were happening and remembering the people that once lived there. Since the death of E. G., Teressa has taken the role of driving Miss Myrth.

Miss Myrth attended the funeral of my mother's youngest sister, Aunt Mabel West-Earls. The graveside funeral and burial was at the Hankins Cemetery near Grubbs, though Aunt Mabel had been away from the area for fifty years or more.

Being eager to greet her, my siblings and I gathered around the graying retired schoolteacher. She was delighted to be remembered and eager to hear our favorite memories of being in her first-grade class. Of all the effort this beloved teacher put into her work, she was surprised to find that she was best remembered by me for the spankings she dispensed. There were many happy days in Miss Myrth's classroom that were uneventful, when everything went smoothly, but those days did not even register in my memory. Making a memory required an incident or an event outside the routine of daily living.

Like antiques, our childhood memories have increased in value and will continue to become more precious as we approach the twilight years in the cycle of life.

There was no preschool or kindergarten class at that time, and neither was there a period of half-day classes to aid in our adjustment to the school schedule. Miss Myrth had her students all day long and had the responsibility of teaching needy children all aspects of socialization: communication skills, self-control, manners, and proper behavior. She gave lots of baby boomers a head start in life before there was an organized Head Start program. She was like a good mother to many little children who spent more time with her each day than with their own busy parents.

Miss Myrth remembers most of her students and says she sees them in her dreams. Each year, she had a photograph taken of her class and recorded the names of her students so she could refresh her memory of them frequently. She said she often dreams that she is still teaching school and feels tremendous frustration due to the inability to cover all the material that she had planned to cover in one term.

"I loved you, little kids," she said.

"How could you love so many children?" I asked

"Because love does not divide, love only multiplies," said the wise teacher.

—∞—

Love Is a Choice

The children of Mary Motes were very fond of each other and stayed close all their adult lives. They didn't write letters or visit often, but they loved one another unconditionally. When they were together again after many years apart, they picked up where they left off.

After many decades, when Tom, Jim, and John Henry retired from their jobs "up North," they moved back to Arkansas. They were blessed to spend a few years with the siblings they had left behind. But when it was time for the men to enter the final stage of life, they had to move away again to be near their children, wherever that might be.

A last hunting trip was planned by the elderly Motes brothers while in their eighties. The gray-haired men readied their firearms and dressed in hunting gear. They walked together into the woods, savoring the familiar sights and sounds. After several minutes of walking on uneven terrain, the others noticed that Jesse, the oldest, was tiring very quickly. Out of concern for him, they all sat down on a sturdy log to let Jesse rest. As the men relived old times, they told their colorful version of hunting trips in the past. The men never mentioned the shaming mistakes of their youth and the limitations and failures of the present. After a couple hours of telling their exploits and sharing memories of their glory days, they rose from the hollow log to head back toward their cars. With gentleness and compassion, they said their heartfelt good-byes knowing there would never be another moment like this. With heavy hearts, they drove to their separate homes. Each brother was an old man who could see the end in sight. Were they exceptional people? No, they were a family who had been blessed to have a loving mother who prayed for them and taught them to practice love and loyalty and to keep the faith.

> Beloved, if God so loved us,
> we ought also to love one another.
>
> —1 John 4:11

Wonderful Words of Life

MARY MOTES WAS A WOMAN who found favor with God. With a large number of children, she died long before her job of mothering was completed. Because we think of death as the worst thing that can happen to a person, it is hard to see God's favor on this mother at first glance.

Most of Mary's children had large families. Several of her children became Christians and their mates also chose to believe on Jesus Christ. Many of Mary's grandchildren and great-grandchildren are active in church work; some are ministers of the Gospel of Jesus Christ. That was God's gift to her. That was her reward. "Lo, children are an heritage of the Lord: and the fruit of the womb is his reward" (Ps. 127:3).

Mabel Margaret Motes Bufford

I believe both my parents were righteous people. They did their best to live right. Righteousness is not recognized by the general population as a positive quality but more often as a peculiarity. Righteous people may not be pursued for their loveable character or their pleasant personalities; they might not be liked or understood by very many people. Righteousness in an individual does not generate popularity. Like faith, righteousness may not be perceived by people but is known to God alone who sees the heart.

Eva and Levi were in no way perfect or remarkable, but the Lord often chose lowly people for His purpose. He partners with the most unlikely people. I have not met two people who were more content than my parents. They liked their life just as it was—peaceful and calm. Though it looked like so little to others, they appreciated all that they had and were thankful to God for it. Dignity seems to shine brightest when it is found in the darkest surroundings.

I knew my parents loved God because they loved the Word of God. The word of the Lord was precious to them. Being anchored in God's word kept them strong in spirit and consistent. They were the same each day whether they were experiencing tragedy or triumph. The Bible was truth, and they kept it close at hand. Tucked under her arm was a Bible that Mama carried almost everywhere she went on the farm. When she walked to the mailbox and had to wait for the mail carrier, she would often sit under the shade of a tree and read the scriptures. When she carried her Bible to the pump for a bucket of water, she would "set a spell" under a tree and read more scriptures.

While growing up, we did not have a regular time of sitting for daily devotions in our home like some Christian families. My parents did not preach to us or require us to read the Bible. We read the Bible because we chose to. Since church was such a delight to us, anything related to church was also a delight.

After church was dismissed on a Sunday morning, my siblings and I gathered the little Sunday school lesson cards, which other children had left behind on the pews and on the floor. The cards had a colorful picture on the front and a Bible story on the back. Since we had so few toys and seldom got anything from the store, those lesson cards were a delight to us. We collected them like other children collected baseball cards, and they are still in our possession today.

Have you ever wondered: What are the most beneficial things I can do to positively affect my family and influence future generations? Some of the most unlikely people discovered spiritual principles in the backwoods that positioned them for God's favor. For those of us who would like to have rewards in this life as well as in the next one, there are three actions that we can take which will result in our being rewarded openly: giving, praying, and fasting (see Matt. 6:4, 6, 18).

A Bible verse that challenges me is Psalms 71:18, "Now also when I am old and grey-headed, O God, forsake me not;

until I have showed thy strength unto this generation, and thy power to everyone that is to come."

Like the five foolish virgins in the Bible story, the baby boom generation fell into apathy because we didn't appreciate what we had in the gospel message. Though we are getting old, we still have a responsibility to this generation. You may ask, "Who am I that I could change anything? There is a great quote by Jane Goodall, "What you do makes a difference, and you have to decide what kind of difference you want to make."

In the Word of God, we are told that our significance was established by God long ago. All lives matter, each person makes a difference, and everyone leaves an impression. We have not known the importance of *one*. In the Word of God, we are told that *one* sinner destroys much good, and there is rejoicing in heaven over *one* sinner who repents.

> I have no greater joy than to hear that
> my children walk in truth.
>
> —3 John 4

19

We'll Understand It Better By and By

As A YOUNG GIRL ENVELOPED in the protective cocoon of the lonely backwoods, I thought poverty was the hindrance to me having a happy life. I was so naïve that I did not realize there were far worse things. Being poor is not the worst thing that can happen to a child.

In Michigan, Sam and I found the prosperity of which we had dreamed. Sam is a retired tool maker from the Cadillac Division of General Motors in Grand Blanc. We have reared four children and helped with grandchildren. I have enjoyed a life of relative ease as a homemaker. I sought employment when I wanted to get out of the house and quit when I tired of the job. We have been blessed with more things than we

Mabel Margaret Motes Bufford

have space for which to store them. We enjoy a country home on twenty acres in a land of plenty. I have found the "different life" that I wanted—an easier life. But happiness is not the result of prosperity.

We have found that the better standard of living has not produced better people of us or of our society; rather, it has resulted in an attitude of cynicism and a sense of disillusionment. The baby boom generation was enticed to buy more and more of the latest electrical gadgets that promised to save us valuable time and create ease. We appreciated the labor-saving devices but saw little advancement and achievement in our extra hours of time saved. I have found that there is little satisfaction in leisure that has been taken without being earned.

I felt ill equipped to handle modern childrearing responsibilities. I hardly knew what aspects of my upbringing to incorporate and what part has become irrelative. Our modern society is now so different that I often feel that I am in foreign territory. Like many older people, I still suffer occasionally from culture shock. I can only hold on to my faith which acts as an anchor in unsettling times.

Though my parents struggled in poverty, they gave to their children—and to future generations—a rich spiritual heritage. "A good man leaveth an inheritance to his children and to his children's children…" (Prov. 13:22). One of the most valuable spiritual lessons I learned from my parents in the backwoods is that faith is more important than riches for faith is riches.

Christian Parenting

My parents never lived above the poverty level. However, they managed to implant their strength of character into their children. Like a birthright, there were values that we could claim: a respect for books, a desire for excellence, and a loyalty to Christian values. With no financial assistance from my parents, two of my brothers have achieved higher education.

While fathers provide and protect, they represent God to their children, and mothers represent the gentle Holy Spirit. In their nurturing, their guidance, and their counseling, mothers are like the Holy Spirit who restrains us from evil pursuits with a tugging sensation that gently nags at our conscience. In our violent world, the most feared creatures on this earth are young adults without a conscience.

It is the Holy Spirit who is the restrainer. He resides deep within us at the core of our being to work from within. In neglecting church attendance and spiritual training, we have made the mistake of expecting our children to be better people without the work of the Holy Spirit than we were with Him.

If we are failing in the harvest of souls for the kingdom of heaven, could it be that we have not prayed as much as we have prepared, we have not travailed as much as we have traveled, we have not fasted as much as we have feasted, nor have we cared as much as we claimed.

Mabel Margaret Motes Bufford

Having relied upon the Holy Spirit, my parents achieved a greater success in parenting than I have. Mama and Daddy had no resources but prayer and involvement in church to help shape the character of their children. Surrounded by godly influence at home and at church, we were kept from many unhealthy influences. Living in the backwoods limited the variety of temptations that others fought regularly. Being poor and extremely shy kept us from mingling with worldly wise individuals and being enticed into questionable pursuits for pleasure.

In this life, we become so earthbound that we cannot see what God is doing or what He has done. From God's vantage point, He can see all the generations that have gone before us and all that will come after us. What my Christian parents called success was the passing of their values to future generations. Even a small adjustment, like an answered prayer, initiates a significant change over a period of many years and several generations. After much time has passed, we can see God's favor on faithful believers who have called upon Him.

From generation to generation, the set changes and characters come and go by way of birth and death. Only God can see the whole picture and understand the plot that covers hundreds of years. Like a seed planted, God begins a work in one generation and brings it to fruition in another. In this way, we make sense of life's hardships and tragedies and give meaning and purpose to that which appears to be unproductive and inconsequential.

Walking with God in the Backwoods

Like a jigsaw puzzle in progress, we live most of our life before we can see the big picture. The early years of our adult life are spent guessing which piece should go where. The longer we work at the puzzle, the more clearly we can see the developing picture and understand its meaning. Change is so gradual that it is best seen over a period of a lifetime. We are often unaware of the changes as they are happening. Hindsight becomes possible only as steady progress has allowed the puzzle pieces to form a clear picture.

As a child, it was too overwhelming to look at the twenty-acre field needing to be hoed, so we just looked at one row. A row of cotton a quarter of a mile long was too overwhelming, so we just looked down. We worked on what was before us and did not think of the cotton field as a whole. This was called "keeping our nose to the grindstone." Finally, when we dared to look back, we were amazed how far we had come. It often takes years before we can rejoice at the difference God has made in us and in our circumstances. A quote by Soren Kierkegaard says, "Life can only be understood backwards; but it must be lived forwards." Sometimes, it takes two or three generations before we can clearly see the favor of God on a family. The good times do not last forever and neither do the difficult times. Change is inevitable for nothing in this life stays the same.

> For the Lord giveth wisdom: out of his mouth
> cometh knowledge and understanding.
>
> —Proverbs 2:6

I'll Live On

The Death of Eva Motes

DEATH APPROACHED MY MOTHER EVER so slowly, giving us time to accept it. First it was colon cancer, then cancer of the liver, and later there was a spot on her lung. She went through all the stages of emotions associated with terminal illness. Little by little, she gave up the disciplines that normally made up her day. She and Daddy had a routine of kneeling in the living room to pray before bedtime. It became a struggle to get up from the floor, and she had to sit to pray while Daddy knelt. She had to stop going for her daily walk for fear that she would fall. She was dying a little at a time as she gave up church attendance, letter writing, journaling, and finally, daily Bible reading.

In mid-January of the year 2000, my mother went to the doctor where she was informed that arrangements should be made for her to start hospice care. She knew what that meant—that she was going to die soon. Though she couldn't say the word *die*, she wanted to know approximately how long she had to live. Mama asked the doctor, "Will I live to see the flowers bloom?"

"Which flowers?" the doctor asked.

Mama didn't answer him for there was nothing more that needed to be said. She knew that death was at the door.

I had planned to spend two weeks caring for my mother before another family member would take a turn. Very calmly, Mama said to me, "If I don't get better while you are here, I'll just pass away." She said it in a matter-of-fact way as if she was in complete control of her destiny and had power over death as well.

By the time death was at her door, my mother showed no fear. She told me, "I just want to slip away quietly." She did not want to linger and be a burden to those she loved. Her greatest concern was for the comfort and convenience of her children.

The Lord allowed Eva Motes to slip away in the early hours of the morning while our side of the world was sleeping. With only her family around the bedside, she departed quietly on February 7, 2000, at the age of eighty-six. Hospice and the funeral home were called, and Mama was taken away under cover of darkness, just the way she wanted it.

Walking with God in the Backwoods

Sorting Stuff

The task of sorting my mother's personal things fell to me and my sister Mildred. Having been a young adult during the Great Depression, my mother was in the habit of saving things others would have thrown away. Mama saved most of the letters that I had written to her for the last thirty-three years since moving to Michigan. I had an urge to read all my letters in case there was interesting things about my children that I had long since forgotten. Mildred knew I had a tendency to keep too much stuff, so she determined to help me to make quick decisions. She opened the letters, skimmed over them, and said, "Nope, there's nothing cute about the kids in this one." I kept very few of the letters.

It seemed that everything my mother had written suddenly became very important to me, and I found it hard to discard anything which she had written. Mildred, on the other hand, is not one to allow clutter and was eager to burn all unnecessary things. I found a scrap of paper with Bible scripture written on it, and I placed it in the pile to save. After the sorting was done, the pile to be saved was much too large, so I sorted through it again to lay aside a little more that could be burned.

After I returned home, I leisurely read the letters and sorted through the pile of papers again. The little scrap of paper with the Bible scripture managed to escape the third burning. As I looked at the thin piece of paper more carefully, I realized that it was the first page of a bible. Only things of great importance are penned on the first page of one's bible. Mama had not only written it in a place of honor but had saved the page when it fell out of the worn bible. In her handwriting, it said,

> Night of 2-7-85
> I have remembered thy name in the night, O Lord.
> At midnight, I will rise to give thanks unto thee.
> It is good for me that I have been afflicted
> that I might learn thy statutes.

Mama must have been in great discomfort and unable to sleep when she penned portions of verses from Psalms 119; they ministered to her. She had prayed and searched the scriptures; she could identify with David the Psalmist for she too was afflicted. The scripture passage had enough significance that she jotted it down in the front of her bible. I took note of the date. It was exactly fifteen years before the date of her death. She passed away in the night on 2-7-2000. Had God granted Mama an extra fifteen years to live as He had done for King Hezekiah? I believe the Lord granted her desire to live and gave her fifteen more years. I also believe the Lord kept me from burning the scrap of paper where she had recorded evidence of that special moment with God. My mother did not mention it to anyone, so it is possible that she was not aware that her prayers had touched the heart of God; we may never know.

Desires of the Heart

According to Psalms 37:4, God promises to give believers the desires of their heart. My mother's desire for herself was that she would be able to live in her own home until she passes away. She did not want to be a burden to anyone, and she did not want to die alone. To provide continuous care, I stayed with Mama for two weeks. She was bedridden for less than one week of that time before her death. The Lord was gracious and allowed her to die in her own bedroom surrounded by her children.

Most of my mother's desires were for her children. God promises to be a "rewarder of those who diligently seek Him" (Heb. 11:6) At the time of her death, my mother was still deeply concerned about the wellbeing of her children and grandchildren. She did not want to leave her offspring with no one to pray for them. How would God respond to this desire? We know our God "is able to do exceeding, abundantly above all that we could ask or think" (Eph. 3:20).

A Spiritual Mother

My phone number was given to Sister Almedia Cheshire by a mutual friend for she and I both needed a friend in our new location near Flint after moving from the suburbs of Detroit. She was an elderly lady in her eighties and suffered isolation in her house where she gave continuous care to her ailing husband.

More than a prayer warrior, Sister Cheshire was an intercessor and became a dear friend to me as the years wore on. She was eager to pray for me and my immediate family, and I valued her help and loving concern. As problems arose with various members of my extended family, I told Sister Cheshire about my concerns for those in Arkansas, and she added their names to her prayer list. We often prayed together when I visited with her and enjoyed one another. She came to know my relatives by the stories I told her and showed eagerness to hear updates on their situation, their problems, and their needs. She took each prayer request seriously and prayed until the answer came. Three years were spent praying for one particular person who was in great peril. One day, I realized that Sister Cheshire had not only been a friend to me, but she had been a friend to my mother, Eva Motes, who she had never met. For years, Sister Cheshire had been praying for me and my sister and brothers (Eva Motes' children). When she prayed for my nieces and nephews and my children, she was praying for Eva Motes' grandchildren.

Walking with God in the Backwoods

Almedia Cheshire had become like a spiritual mother. God had given my mother one of the best friend she could have—one who would intercede for the family she left behind. A mother can have no greater friend than one who will pray for her children and grandchildren.

Later, I realized that my friend, Sister Cheshire, had not only been a friend to my mother long after Eva Motes had passed away, but she was being a friend to Mary Motes who died long before I was born. When Sister Cheshire prayed for me, she was not only praying for Eva's daughter but also for Mary Motes' granddaughter. When she prayed for my children, she was praying for Eva Motes' grandchildren and Mary Motes' great-grandchildren. I told Sister Cheshire about Mildred's little granddaughter, Destiny, who had lost her mother to cystic fibrosis and came to live with Mildred at seven years old. While Sister Cheshire was praying for Mildred's granddaughter, she was in reality praying for Eva Motes' great-grandchild and Mary Motes' great-great-grandchild. God is so good to arrange such a reward for those two ladies who found favor in His sight many generations ago.

Isolation and loneliness were Sister Cheshire's most common complaint. She had health problems that kept her housebound. Great faith in God gave her a "never give up" attitude that refused to accept limitations. Sister Cheshire made the best of her situation by giving herself to prayer and intercession. She called it her "rocking chair ministry."

Neither my mother nor my spiritual mother achieved social acceptance; both had often been devalued. As it is with some great artist, the extent of their exceptional ability is not recognized until long after they are gone. Many years may pass before the overall picture takes focus and their glaring faults and personality flaws cease to demand preeminence. My friend, Sister Cheshire, suffered with dementia and died at the age of ninety-two.

—⚉—

Grieved Parents

Though he could not hear what was being said, Daddy continued to attend church. He enjoyed seeing the familiar faces of the people he loved and feeling the presence of God. Daddy lived two years without Mama while he dealt with sorrow and loneliness. His hearing loss separated him from people and sentenced him to a world of silence. Like Abram, in the Bible, Daddy found the Lord was his "exceeding, great reward" (Gen. 15:1).

There was one desire of Eva and Levi's heart that they did not live to see fulfilled. They wanted all their children to attend church and serve the Lord. Though one of their grown children, Mildred and her husband, did not attend church, they were believers in Jesus Christ.

Mildred always had a house full of children to care for and huge gardens that needed to be planted and tended and vegetables that needed to be picked. Being inundated with perishable vegetables and the time-consuming job of home canning, the demands on her often left her overwhelmed. On the occasions that she had leisure time, when the work was completed, she worked on piecing a quilt top. There just didn't seem to be enough time for church attendance.

Bill worked hard and always had so much to do around his property. Church just did not appeal to him as the way to spend his much-deserved downtime.

Our parents, Eva and Levi, understood the situation and were sympathetic, yet they were grieved for thirty years that their prayers for their daughter and her family to attend church had not been answered. Mildred and Bill eventually became faithful in church attendance. They still had lots of chores to complete and a house full of children to care for, but God gave them a motivating factor—a special visitation of His Holy Spirit. Their circumstances did not change but their priorities changed.

—m—

The Death of Levi Motes

On April 13, 2002, at the age of ninety-one, Daddy died in a head-on collision. He was gone in an instant. He, too, had been granted the desire of his heart to live in his own home until the end. We found his coffee cup and his plate still on the kitchen table where he had eaten the eggs he had fried for breakfast that morning. If he had known he would not be returning, he probably would have washed the dishes before he left. If he had known it would be his last day on earth, he would have stayed at home. On that day, he drove to Beebe with a small chicken coop in the backseat of his car with the intention of buying a few chickens at the sale barn. It is interesting that his destination was the same town on that day in 2002 that it had been in 1920 when his family first came to Arkansas. His interest in caring for chickens showed us Daddy was making plans for the immediate future and expected to remain active until the very end. He was the type of man who wouldn't mind dying alone and would prefer to die with his work boots on. I felt so bad about the fatal accident that brought grief to another family as well. He would never want to be a burden on his family or bring harm to another. At his funeral, Rev. Vince Vire quoted a scripture that gave me great comfort. He said, "Death is not an accident. Death is an appointment, for 'it is appointed unto men once to die'" (Heb. 9:27).

"We're the old folks now," Mike said to his siblings with a tone of resignation. With the death of both parents comes the "changing of the guard." As it is in a relay race, the baton has been passed to the next generation. Though our parents are gone, their influence remains.

The Comforter Comes

In the days after Daddy's funeral, Mildred and her husband planned a work day at the little house that had been our parents' home. All the out-of-state visitors had gone back to their busy lives of work and family and left Mildred and Bill to work alone to empty the house. They spent most of the day carrying discarded things to the burn pile. They were weary and filled with grief as they made the hard and final decisions about each item they picked up. Every little thing represented the proof of Mama and Daddy's very existence. To burn our parents' things was like erasing the evidence that they had ever been there.

As Bill walked toward the burn pile, he spotted a white dove sitting calmly on a branch in a little pecan tree nearby. The dove was watching the two of them as they walked past. They had never seen a white dove around there before, and supposed that it had come from another area. The dove sat for nearly an hour with his head turning slowly to allow his gaze to follow them as they walked back and forth. Mildred and Bill were comforted as they glanced toward the dove every few minutes as they walked by. They remembered having heard the song "On the Wings of a Dove" and the story of the Holy Spirit descending from heaven in the form of a dove. Slowly, it dawned on them that Jesus had promised to send the Holy Spirit to earth and called Him the "Comforter" (see John 14:26). It was a special moment when they realized the

Lord had sent the dove to comfort them when their grief was at the height of human endurance. The Lord has made a promise to all who trust in Him for the hardest time of our life or the saddest day. I don't know in what form he will choose to come to you, but he will come, and it will be comforting when you recognize Him.

I will not leave you comfortless. I will come to you.

—John 14:18

Walking with God in the Backwoods

Songs

Favorite Songs and Hymns

Stamps-Baxter Music & Printing Co., Inc.

Dallas, Texas 75208; Pangburn, Arkansas 72121; Chattanooga, Tennessee 37404

Copyright 1939, by Stamps-Baxter Music and Printing Co., Inc.

"Where He Leads" by W. A. Ogden
"Tell Me the Old, Old Story" by W. H. Doan
"Amazing Grace"
"I'll Be List'ning" by V. O. Stamps
"The Old-Time Religion"
"Gathering Home" by R. M. McIntosh
"When the Saints Go Marching In" by Luther G. Presley, Virgil O. Stamps
"No Tears in Heaven" by Robert S. Arnold
"Hold to God's Unchanging Hand" by Jennie Wilson, F. L. Eiland, and Clyde Williams
"When the Roll Is Called Up Yonder" by James Black
"I'll Fly Away" by Albert E. Brumley
"This World Is Not My Home" by Albert E. Brumley
"I'll Meet You in the Morning" by Albert E. Brumley
"Love Lifted Me" by Howard E. Smith
"Wonderful Words of Life" by P. P. Bliss
"I'll Live On" by Thos. J. Laney

Mabel Margaret Motes Bufford

Church Hymnal

Shaped Notes Only
Tennessee Music and Printing Company, Cleveland, Tennessee
Copyright 1951, by Tennessee Music and Printing Company

"That Glad Reunion Day" by Adger M. Pace
"A New Name in Glory" by C. Austin Miles
"Where Could I Go?" by J. B. Coats
"We'll Understand It Better By and By" by R. E. Winsett

CPSIA information can be obtained at www.ICGtesting.com
Printed in the USA
BVOW06s0757050716

454188BV00002B/2/P